Topics for Today

An Advanced Reading Skills Text

Second Edition

Topics for Today

An Advanced Reading Skills Text

Second Edition

Lorraine C. Smith
Nancy Nici Mare

English Language Institute
Queens College
The City University of New York

Illustrations by
Joseph Tenga

Heinle & Heinle Publishers

I(T)P   A Division of International Thomson Publishing, Inc.
Boston, Massachusetts 02116 U.S.A.

Pacific Grove • Albany • Bonn • Boston • Cincinnati • Detroit • London • Madrid • Melbourne
Mexico City • New York • Paris • San Francisco • Tokyo • Toronto • Washington

The publication of *Topics for Today, Second Edition* was directed by members of the Newbury House Publishing Team at Heinle & Heinle:

Erik Gundersen, **Editorial Director**
Bruno R. Paul, **Market Development Director**
Kristin Thalheimer, **Production Services Coordinator**
Stanley Galek, **Vice President and Publisher, ESL**

Also participating in the publication of this program were:
Project Manager: LeGwin Associates
Associate Editor: Ken Pratt
Associate Market Development Director: Mary Sutton
Production Editor: Maryellen Eschmann Killeen
Manufacturing Coordinator: Mary Beth Hennebury
Cover Designer: Kim Wedlake
Photo/Video Specialist: Jonathan Stark

Heinle & Heinle Publishers
20 Park Plaza
Boston, MA 02116 USA

International Thomson Publishing
Berkshire House 168-173
High Holborn
London WC1V 7AA
England

Thomas Nelson Australia
102 Dodds Street
South Melbourne, 3205
Victoria, Australia

Nelson Canada
1120 Birchmount Road
Scarborough, Ontario
Canada M1K 5G1

International Thomson Publishing Gmbh
Konigwinterer Strasse 418
53227 Bonn
Germany

International Thomson Publishing Asia
Block 311 Henderson Road #08-03
Henderson Industrial Park
Singapore 0315

International Thomson Publishing-Japan
Hirakawacho-cho Kyowa Building, 3F
2-2-1 Hirakawacho-cho
Chiyoda-ku, 102 Tokyo
Japan

International Thomson Editores
Campos Eliseos 385, Piso 7
Col. Polanco
11560 Mexico DF., Mexico

International Thomson Editores
Iberoamerica
Magallanes 25
28015 Madrid, Spain

All art and illustration by Joseph Tenga except as noted below:

p. 1: © Jeff Greenberg/The Image Works
p. 67: © Mark C. Burnett/Photo Researchers Inc.
p. 80: Jonathan Stark/Heinle and Heinle
p. 101: Jonathan Stark/Heinle and Heinle
p. 106: © Drs. T. Ried & D. Ward/Peter Arnold, Inc.
p. 119: © Millennium Pharmaceuticals, Inc.
p. 127: © 1995 Robert Burke/Liasion International
p. 141: Jonathan Stark/Heinle and Heinle
p. 166: © Cindy Darby/San Gabriel Valley Tribune

p. 181: © Per Breiehagen/Time Magazine
p. 191: ©John H. Meehan 1980/Photo Researchers, Inc.
p. 205: © Karl Weidmann/Photo Researchers, Inc.
p. 225: © Tom & Pat Leeson/Photo Researchers, Inc.
p. 230: © U.S. Department of Energy/Science Photo Library/Photo Researchers, Inc.
p. 238: © Blair Seitz/Photo Researchers, Inc.

Dictionary facsimiles from *Merriam-Webster's Collegiate® Dictionary, Tenth Edition* © 1996, reproduced here with permission from Merriam-Webster Inc.

Copyright © 1997 by Heinle & Heinle Publishers
A division of International Thomson Publishing, Inc.

Library of Congress Cataloging-in-Publication Data
Smith, Lorraine C.
    Topics for today : an advanced reading skills text / Lorraine C. Smith, Nancy Nici Mare : illustrations by Joseph Tenga. — 2nd ed.
        p. cm.
    Includes index.
    ISBN 0-8384-5216-7
    1. English language—Textbooks for foreign speakers. 2. Current events—Problems, exercises, etc. 3. Readers—Current events.
I. Mare. Nancy Nici.   II. Title
PE1128.S5853   1996
428.6'4—dc21   96-50296
                                                                                  CIP

ISBN: 0-8384-5216-7

1 2 3 4 5 6 7 8 9 10

To Elizabeth

Acknowledgments

Our gratitude and respect goes to our editor, Erik Gundersen, for his generosity of spirit and his insights, which have contributed to the success of our series. For all our friends at the ELI, and to our families, many thanks for their ongoing help, interest, and support.

L.C.S. and N.N.M.

Contents

Preface

Topics for Today, Second Edition is an ESL/EFL reading skills text intended for advanced, college-bound students. The passages in this book are original articles from periodicals and newspapers. Some have been shortened slightly, but none have been simplified; consequently, the students have the opportunity to read actual selections from a variety of publications. The topics are fresh and timely. The issues are global in nature. Experience has shown that college-bound students are interested in modern topics of a more academic nature than is often found in ESL/EFL texts. They need extensive reading in the styles of writing and the vocabulary that they will actually encounter during their university studies. This book provides them with this essential practice. It requires students to not only read an article, but also to extract information from various forms of charts, graphs, and illustrations.

Topics for Today is one in a series of reading skill texts. The complete series has been designed to meet the needs of students from the beginning to the advanced levels and includes the follwing:

- *Themes for Today*   beginning
- *Insights for Today*   high beginning
- *Issues for Today*   intermediate
- *Concepts for Today*   high intermediate
- *Topics for Today*   advanced

Topics for Today, Second Edition has been designed for flexible use by teachers and students. The text consists of four units, each containing three chapters that deal with related subjects. Each chapter contains a main reading passage and a related reading. At the same time, each chapter is entirely separate in content from the other chapters contained in that unit. This approach gives teachers and students the option of either completing all three chapters in a unit, in any order they wish, or of choosing individual chapters as a focus in class.

The prereading preparation before each reading helps activate the students' background knowledge of the topic and encourages students to think about the ideas, facts, and vocabulary that will be presented. The exercises and activities that follow the reading passage are intended to develop and improve vital skills, including identifying main idea and supporting details, summary writing, overall reading proficiency, inferencing ability, learning vocabulary from context, using the dictionary appropriately, and critical thinking. The activities give students the opportunity to master useful vocabulary encountered in the articles through discussion and group work and lead the students through general comprehension of main ideas and specific information. Equally important, the text provides the students with regular opportunities to reflect on how the reading strategies they use helps them improve their overall reading proficiency.

As the students interact with the text, they will improve their skills and develop confidence in their ability to understand new material. At the same time, they and their teacher will be able to observe their steady progress towards skillful, independent reading.

New to the Second Edition

While *Topics for Today* retains the overall format of the first edition, the authors have made several significant changes to the original book. *Topics for Today, Second Edition* comprises twelve chapters, three chapters in each of four units. The second edition contains six new chapters: "Dressing for Success," "My Husband, the Outsider," "My Genes Made Me Do it," "Assisted Suicide: Multiple Perspectives," "The Gift of Life: When One body Can Save Another," and "A Nuclear Graveyard." In addition, several of the original readings have been updated to reflect new information. Furthermore, each chapter includes a second reading that relates to the topic of the main reading, and provides another perspective on the subject matter of that chapter. These revisions have been designed to provide students with more extensive reading practice.

Topics for Today, Second Edition contains an enhanced Prereading Preparation section, which provides more thoughtful, motivating questions, readings, and activities. The second edition includes improved graphics, which are designed both to enhance students' comprehension of information processed in graphs and to facilitate understanding of the text they relate to. The Outlining Skills Practice has been redesigned. The new Reading Overview: Main Idea, Details, and Summary exercise provides practice in distinguishing between and writing a main idea and a summary, and includes outlines, charts and flowcharts, depending on each reading and the type of information it contains. Furthermore, the Reading Overview design takes into account students' different learning and organizational styles. The new Follow-up Activities section contains a variety of activities, and provides more opportunities for student interaction. It also contains a Reading Strategies Checklist, which is designed to help students become more aware of and reflect on their reading strategies. Moreover, *Topics for Today, Second Edition* has a Topics for Discussion and Writing section, which includes questions for journal writing, providing even more opportunities for students to incorporate writing as a natural part of reading.

The second edition has end-of-unit crossword puzzles, which provide a review of the vocabulary encountered in all three chapters of each unit.

All of these revisions and enhancements to *Topics for Today, Second Edition* have been designed to help students improve their reading skills, to develop confidence as they work through the text, and to prepare them for academic work.

Introduction

How to Use This Book

Every chapter in this book consists of the following:

Prereading Preparation
Reading Passage
Reading Overview: Main Idea, Details, and Summary
Statement Evaluation
Reading Analysis
Dictionary Skills
Critical Thinking
Another Perspective
Follow-up Activities
Topics for Discussion and Writing

The second reading in each chapter (Another Perspective) may be part of the Prereading Preparation in order to provide background knowledge for the main reading of the chapter or to provide the readers with the opportunity to consider certain perspectives on the main reading. The second reading may also be found later in the chapter, where it provides another perspective on the topic of the main reading.

There is a Crossword Puzzle at the end of each unit. An Index of Key Words and Phrases and an Answer Key are located at the end of the book.

The format of each chapter in the book is consistent. Some activities, by their nature, involve pair and group work. Other exercises may be assigned for homework. This choice, of course, depends on the individual teacher's preference, as well as the availability of class time.

Prereading Preparation

The prereading activities vary throughout the text, depending on the subject matter. This section is designed to stimulate student interest and generate vocabulary relevant to the passage. The students should consider the source of the article, relate the topic to their own experience, and try to predict what they are going to read about.

The Reading Passage

Research has demonstrated the value of multiple readings, especially where each reading serves a specific purpose. The students will read each passage several times. As the students read the passage for the first time, for example, they should be encouraged to identify main ideas. During the second reading, they will identify supporting details. At the third reading, students can focus on unfamiliar vocabulary as they work through the Reading Analysis and Dictionary Skills.

Reading Overview: Main Idea, Details, and Summary

In this exercise, students are asked to read the passage a second time and take notes based in part on the main ideas they identified during their first reading. The teacher may want to review the concept of main idea, notetaking, and summarizing before beginning the exercise. The Details outline, chart, or flowchart can be sketched by the teacher on the blackboard and completed by individual students in front of the class. Variations can be discussed by the class as a group. It should be pointed out to the students that in American colleges, teachers often base their exams on the notes that the students are expected to take during class lectures. When the students have finished notetaking, they are asked to briefly summarize the passage.

Statement Evaluation

After reading, taking notes, and summarizing the passage, the students will read a series of statements and check whether each is true, false, an opinion, an inference, or not mentioned in the reading. This activity can be done individually or in pairs. Students should be encouraged to discuss the reasons for their choices.

Reading Analysis

The students will read each question and answer it. This exercise deals with vocabulary from context, transition words, punctuation clues, sentence structure, and sentence comprehension. It may be helpful for students to read the passage again as they work through this exercise. The Reading Analysis exercise is effective when done in pairs because students have an opportunity to discuss their responses.

Dictionary Skills

The entries in this section have been taken from *Merrriam-Webster's Collegiate Dictionary, Tenth Edition*. This exercise provides the students with much needed practice in selecting the appropriate dictionary entry for an unknown word. The students are given a dictionary entry for one of the words in the text. One or more sentences containing the unknown word are provided above the entry. The student reads the entry and selects the appropriate one, given the context provided. Students need to understand that this is not always a clear process; some entries are very similar, and it could be that more than one entry is appropriate if the context is general. They should aim for the nearest in meaning rather than absolute correctness. The students can work in pairs on this exercise and report back to the class. They should be prepared to justify their choice.

Critical Thinking

For this activity, the students refer back to parts of the article, think about the implications of the information or comments that are contained, and consider the author's purpose and tone. The goal of the exercise is for the students to form their own ideas and opinions on aspects of the topic discussed. The students can work on these questions as an individual writing exercise or orally as a small group discussion activity. In this activity, students are encouraged to use the vocabulary they have been learning.

Another Perspective

The second reading in the chapters provides another point of view, or an additional topic, related to the main reading. The students should focus on general comprehension, on relating this reading to the primary reading, and on considering the ideas and information as they engage in the Follow-up Activities and Topics for Discussion and Writing.

Follow-up Activities

The first item in the Follow-up activities is a *Self-Evaluation of Reading Strategies.* The purpose of this self-evaluation is to help students become more aware of the strategies they use to help themselves understand written material. It is a personal, reflective activity, and progress should be judged by the students themselves. At the same time, students should be encouraged to utilize these strategies in all their reading.

The remainder of each section contains a variety of activities, some intended for in-class work, others as out-of-class assignments. Some activities are designed for pair and small group work. Students are encouraged to use the information and vocabulary from the passages both orally and in writing.

Topics for Discussion and Writing

In this section, students are encouraged to use the information and vocabulary from the passage both orally and in writing. The writing assignments may be done entirely in class, begun in class and finished at home, or done at home. The last activity in this section is a journal-writing assignment that provides the students with an opportunity to reflect on the topic in the chapter and respond to it in some personal way. Students should be encouraged to keep a journal, and to write in it regularly. The students' journal writing may be purely personal, or the students may choose to have the teacher read them.

Crossword Puzzle

The crossword puzzles are located at the end of each unit. They provide a review of the vocabulary in the chapters in the given unit. They may be done in pairs, as a homework assignment, or as an optional enrichment activity.

Index of Key Words and Phrases

This section contains important words and phrases from all the chapters for easy reference. It is located after the last chapter.

Answer Key

The Answer Key is located at the end of the book and provides the answers for the exercises. The Answer Key should be considered a resource for students and teachers alike. For example, if the students are initially having difficulty in the Reading Overview, they may want to look at the main idea, details, and summaries for the first few chapters as models. In addition, if they are working on the Dictionary Skills, they may not always see the reason why one entry is more appropriate than another. The Answer Key provides some explanations for ambiguous entries.

Society:
School and Family

Dressing for Success

• Prereading Preparation

1. The Long Beach, California school district has had a dress code for more than a decade, but in 1994 it became the first in the nation to adopt a districtwide K–8 uniform policy. The following is the district's K–8 dress code:

   a. Students must be clean.
   b. No oversized or sagging clothing.
   c. No open-toed shoes or sandals.
   d. No jewelry that could cause injury.
   e. No beepers or pagers.
   f. No hats, unless part of a school uniform or medically required.
   g. No sunglasses in class unless medically required.

   Work with a partner. What kinds of clothes do you think elementary and high school students should be allowed to wear? What kinds of clothes should be banned? Fill in the chart below. You may choose items from the list above or add your own.

Clothes Allowed	Clothes Banned

3

2. Work in small groups. Choose two items from your list of clothes that should be banned. On the lines below, explain why these items should not be worn in school.

   a. _____

   _____

   b. _____

   _____

3. On the blackboard, write your choices of clothes that should be banned. As a class, compare your combined list with the list from the Long Beach school district. Do you agree with its list? Why or why not? As a class, decide which three items you would ban.

4. Read the title of this article. What do you think this passage will be about?

Dressing for Success

by Jessica Portner
Education Week

1   Linda Moore has been feeling especially proud lately. And she has President Clinton to thank.

    In his State of the Union Address last month, Mr. Clinton praised student uniforms as a way to promote
5   safety and discipline in public schools. Ms. Moore, the principal of Will Rogers Middle School here, felt a particular satisfaction in the endorsement.

    "Everybody is looking for answers, and here is a district that is doing something that is working," she said.
10   For more than a year, the 83,000-student Long Beach system has required its elementary and middle school students to dress in uniform fashion. It was the first public school district in the nation to do so.

    Mr. Clinton may have had this Southern California
15   school system in mind when, in his speech, he challenged public schools to mandate uniforms "if it meant that teenagers (would) stop killing each other over designer jackets."

20   ### Dramatic Results

    Since the mandatory-uniform policy was launched in 56 elementary and 14 middle schools here in fall

Reprinted with permission from *Education Week*, Vol. XV No. 31, February 14, 1996.

1994, violence and discipline problems have decreased dramatically, a recent survey by the district shows.

25 From the year before uniforms were required, 1993–94, to last year, assault and battery cases in grades K–8 have dropped 34 percent. Physical fights between students have dropped by 51 percent, and there were 32 percent fewer suspensions.

30 Though each school in the district can choose its own uniform, most Long Beach students are required to wear black or blue pants, skirts or shorts with white shirts. Nearly 60,000 K–8 students are affected by the policy.

Parents have the option of excusing their children 35 from the requirement. But, so far, only 500 parents have filled out petitions to exempt their children, according to Dick Van DerLaan, a spokesman for the district.

In addition to Long Beach, a few other districts in 40 California and across the country are testing the benefits of requiring students to come to school in color-specific, and sometimes style-specific, clothing.

The Oakland, Calif. schools began a similar uniform policy last September. And a small number of other 45 districts—including Dade County, Florida; Seattle, Washington; and Charleston, South Carolina—allow schools to decide for themselves whether to require uniforms.

But Long Beach appears to be the first school sys-50 tem to have documented measurable success in improving student behavior.

Since students at Rogers Middle School started wearing black bottoms, white tops, and red jackets or sweaters, fights have declined by 40 percent, and aca-55 demic performance has improved, school officials said.

Uniforms are an effective method of reducing unwanted behavior, Ms. Moore said, because the more formal clothing puts students in the right mind-set to learn.

"It's about dressing for success," said Ms. Moore, 60 who said she wears the school uniform as a gesture of solidarity with her students. She has a selection of bright red blazers in her home closet.

Not one parent at Rogers Middle School has opted out of the plan this year, and a quick look around cam-65 pus at the unbroken stream of red, white, and black shows that students are largely compliant. But there are some exceptions.

"Tuck in that shirt," she called out to one dishev-
eled teenager who was slouching against a locker. She
70 looked disparagingly at another whose sweatshirt was
clearly purple, not red.

In addition to choosing uniform colors, each of the
district's schools is allowed to choose the fabric and
style of dress. One elementary school requires its pu-
75 pils to wear ties, and a few others prefer plaid, but
most stick with blue or black and white.

"This isn't a private, prep school with a coat-of-
arms and saddle shoes look," Mr. Van DerLaan said.
"It's a little more California casual."
80

Generation Gap

When Judy Jacob had two children attending Rogers
Middle School, she was among the organizers of the effort to bring uniforms to that school. She now has a child
85 in a district elementary school and has remained enthusi-
astic about uniforms. "There are so few boundaries for
kids these days, with the drug use and violence, so if we
can give them some limits, that's good," she said.

The uniformity tends to bolster safety because it
90 makes it easier to spot people who may not belong on
campus, school leaders say.

But a large portion of the district's students aren't
as upbeat as parents and teachers appear to be. And
the older they get, the less they seem to like it—which
95 may not bode well for talk in the district of expanding
the uniform requirement to high schools.

"It's like we're all in jail," said Hector Gonzalez, a
7th grader at Rogers.

Alicia Nunez, an 8th grader at Franklin Middle
100 School, complained that the regimented attire stifles
her creativity. "You come to school to get your education, not for them to tell you how to dress," the 14-
year-old said as she strode across campus wearing a
chocolate-brown T-shirt and jeans.
105

Legal Challenge

The U.S. Supreme Court hasn't directly addressed
the question of whether public schools can impose
dress requirements on their students. Lower courts,
110 however, have generally upheld school dress codes.

Last fall, in one of the first legal tests of a mandatory uniform policy, an Arizona state judge upheld a

Phoenix middle school's policy, even though it does not give students the right to opt out of the requirement.

115   Most public schools and districts offer a parent or guardian the opportunity to excuse a child from wearing a uniform. And most do not impose harsh penalties on students who are supposed to wear uniforms but don't.

"Schools generally feel they need to exercise lati-
120 tude when they put their foot down," said Gary Marx, a spokesman for the American Association of School Administrators in Arlington, Virginia.

The American Civil Liberties Union of Southern California, on behalf of a group of low-income families,
125 filed a lawsuit in state court last October against the Long Beach Unified School District, claiming that the district's uniform policy is a financial burden on poor families. The ACLU also claimed that the district has violated state law by neglecting to adequately inform
130 parents about their right to exempt their children from the program.

The law signed in 1994 by California Gov. Pete Wilson to allow state public schools to require uniforms also says that parents must have a way to opt out of
135 such requirements.

The ACLU lawyers say many parents can't afford the cost of school uniforms. About 66 percent of the district's elementary and middle school students qualify for free or reduced-price lunches. The case is
140 currently in mediation.

Hope Carradine, who dresses three of her five children in uniforms, said she had to ask other family members to pay for them. "I shop thrift and buy in bulk; you can't do that with uniforms," she said.
145

Other Strategies

But district officials say that parents can buy the essential items—a white shirt and a pair of pants—for $25 from several area stores. In addition, many
150 schools sell sweatshirts or shorts for $6 each. Many local charities also provide free uniforms, backpacks, and shoes to needy students.

And if parents find the costs too burdensome, Mr. Van DerLaan, the district spokesman, said, they can al-
155 ways opt out. A flier explaining this right was sent to parents nine months before any uniform policies became effective, he said.

Despite their commitment to the school-uniform policy, Long Beach officials don't view it as a panacea
160 for discipline problems.

Other efforts, such as stepped-up parent involvement and additional conflict-resolution classes, also have contributed to the more peaceful climate on campuses, school leaders here say.

165 The district is continuing to evaluate the benefits of uniforms to determine whether last year's improved numbers for behavior were more than a blip on the screen.

And while some Long Beach students complain that
170 the regulation dress is monotonous and dampens their personal style, many also see a positive side.

"The good thing is people judge you on your inner characteristics rather than what you wear," said Nick Duran, an 8th grader and the student-body president
175 at Rogers Middle School. "Plus," he said, "it's easier to choose what to put on in the morning."

• A. Reading Overview: Main Idea, Details, and Summary

Read the passage again. As you read, underline what you think are the most important ideas in the reading. Then, in one or two sentences, write the main idea of the reading. *Use your own words.*

Main idea:

_____

_____

_____

Details:

Use the chart below to organize the arguments for and against requiring uniforms in school. Indicate who gave each opinion. Refer back to the information you underlined in the passage as a guide. When you have finished, write a brief summary of the reading. *Use your own words.*

Dressing for Success

School Uniform Dress Code	
Arguments in Favor	**Arguments against**

Summary:

_____

_____

_____

_____

• B. Statement Evaluation

Read the following statements. Then scan the article again quickly to find out if each sentence is **True (T), False (F),** or an **Inference (I).**

1. _____ Violence in Long Beach schools has increased since the uniform policy began.

2. _____ President Clinton believes that public school uniforms lead to a safer school environment.

3. _____ Some teenagers have killed each other for their designer jackets.

4. _____ All Long Beach parents must allow their children to wear uniforms.

5. _____ The decrease in violence and discipline problems is a result of the school uniform policy.

6. _____ According to district officials, the essential school uniform items are not expensive.

• C. Reading Analysis

Read each question carefully. Either circle the letter or number of the correct answer, or write your answer in the space provided.

1. a. Read lines 3–7. What did the President endorse?

   1. safety in public schools
   2. discipline in public schools
   3. a dress code in public schools

   b. **endorsement** means

   1. discipline
   2. support
   3. disagreement

2. Read lines 8–24. In line 21, **mandatory uniform policy** means uniforms are

a. optional
b. required
c. important

3. Read lines 34–38.

a. What **option** do the parents have?

_____

_____

b. An **option** is

1. a choice
2. a decision
3. a requirement

4. Read lines 39–46. In line 43–44, what is the Oakland schools' **similar uniform policy?**

_____

_____

5. Read lines 63–67. **"Not one parent . . . has opted out of the plan"** means

a. all the parents agreed to have their children obey the dress code
b. none of the parents agreed to have their children obey the dress code

6. Read lines 82–88. What is a synonym for **boundaries?**

_____

7. Read lines 92–96: **"And the older they get, the less they seem to like it. . . ."** Who likes the dress code more?

a. older students
b. younger students

8. a. Read lines 97 and 98. Does this student like the dress code?

_____

b. How do you know?

_____

_____

9. Read lines 123–131. Why might the uniform policy be a **financial burden?**

_____

10. Read lines 158–164.

   a. Do Long Beach officials believe the dress code is a **panacea** for discipline problems? _____

   b. What else has contributed to the decrease in violence in schools?

_____

_____

   c. **Panacea** means

     1. cure
     2. requirement
     3. cause

   d. **Stepped-up** means

     1. hard
     2. higher
     3. increased

• D. Dictionary Skills

Read the dictionary entry for each word, and consider the context of the sentence from the passage. Write the number of the definition that is appropriate for the context on the line next to the word. Be prepared to explain your choice.

1. From the year before uniforms were required, 1993–94, to last year, assault and battery **cases** in grades K–8 have dropped 34 percent.

   case: _____

   case \'kās\ *n* [ME *cas,* fr. OF, fr. L *casus* fall, chance, fr. *cadere* to fall — more at CHANCE] (13c)   **1 a :** a set of circumstances or conditions ⟨is the statement true in all three ~s⟩   **b (1) :** a situation requiring investigation or action (as by the police)   **(2) :** the object of investigation or consideration   **2 :** CONDITION; *specif* : condition of body or mind   **3** [ME *cas,* fr. MF, fr. L *casus,* trans. of Gk *ptōsis,* lit., fall]   **a** : an inflectional form of a noun, pronoun, or adjective indicating its grammatical relation to other words   **b** : such a relation whether indicated by inflection or not   **4 :** what actually exists or happens : FACT   **5 a :** a suit or action in law or equity   **b (1) :** the evidence supporting a conclusion or judgment   **(2) :** ARGUMENT; *esp* : a convincing argument   **6 a :** an instance of disease or injury; *also* : PATIENT   **b** : an instance that directs attention to a situation or exhibits it in action : EXAMPLE   **c :** a peculiar person : CHARACTER   **7 :** oneself considered as an object of harassment ⟨get off my ~⟩   *syn* see INSTANCE — **in any case** : without regard to or in spite of other considerations : whatever else is done or is the case ⟨war is inevitable *in any case*⟩ ⟨*in any case* the report will be made public next month⟩

2. Since the mandatory-uniform policy was **launched** in 56 elementary and 14 middle schools in fall 1994, violence and discipline problems have decreased dramatically.

   launch: _____

   launch \'lȯnch, 'länch\ *vb* [ME, fr. ONF *lancher,* fr. LL *lanceare* to wield a lance — more at LANCE] *vt* (14c)   **1 a :** to throw forward : HURL   **b :** to release, catapult, or send off (a self-propelled object) ⟨~ a rocket⟩   **2 a :** to set (a boat or ship) afloat   **b :** to give (a person) a start ⟨~ed in a new career⟩   **c (1) :** to originate or set in motion : INITIATE, INTRODUCE   **(2) :** to get off to a good start   ~ *vi* **1 a :** to spring forward : TAKE OFF   **b :** to throw oneself energetically : PLUNGE   **2 a** *archaic* : to slide down the ways   **b :** to make a start

Pronunciation Guide

\ə\ **abut**   \ʼ\ **kitten,** F **table**   \ər\ **further**   \a\ **ash**   \ā\ **ace**   \ä\ **mop, mar**
\au̇\ **out**   \ch\ **chin**   \e\ **bet**   \ē\ **easy**   \g\ **go**   \i\ **hit**   \ī\ **ice**   \j\ **job**
\ŋ\ **sing**   \ō\ **go**   \ȯ\ **law**   \ȯi\ **boy**   \th\ **thin**   \t̲h̲\ **the**   \ü\ **loot**   \u̇\ **foot**
\y\ **yet**   \zh\ **vision**   \ȧ, k̲, ⁿ, œ, œ̄, ue, ūe, ʸ\

3. Parents have the **option** of excusing their children from the requirement. But, so far, only 500 parents have filled out petitions to exempt their children. In fact, not one parent at Rogers Middle School has opted out of the plan this year.

option: _____

op•tion \'äp-shən\ *n* [F, fr. L *option-, optio* free choice; akin to L *optare* to choose] (ca. 1604)   **1** : an act of choosing   **2 a** : the power or right to choose : freedom of choice   **b** : a privilege of demanding fulfillment of a contract on any day within a specified time   **c** : a contract conveying a right to buy or sell designated securities, commodities, or property interest at a specified price during a stipulated period; *also* : the right conveyed by an option   **d** : a right of an insured person to choose the form in which payments due on a policy shall be made or applied   **3** : something that may be chosen: as   **a** : an alternative course of action ⟨didn't have many ∼s open⟩   **b** : an item that is offered in addition to or in place of standard equipment   **4** : an offensive football play in which a back may choose whether to pass or run with the ball — called also *option play*   *syn* see CHOICE

4. The U.S. Supreme Court hasn't directly addressed the question of whether public schools can impose dress requirements on their students. Lower courts, however, have generally **upheld** school dress codes.

   Last fall, in one of the first legal tests of a mandatory uniform policy, an Arizona state judge **upheld** a Phoenix middle school's policy, even though it does not give students the right to opt out of the requirement.

uphold: _____

up•hold \(ˌ)əp-'hōld\ *vt* **-held** \-'held\; **-hold•ing** (13c)   **1 a** : to give support to   **b** : to support against an opponent   **2 a** : to keep elevated   **b** : to lift up   *syn* see SUPPORT — **up•hold•er** *n*

• E. Critical Thinking

Read each question carefully. Write your response in the space provided. Remember that there is no one correct answer. Your response depends on what **you** think.

1. Refer to your list of arguments in favor of and against the school uniform requirement in the reading. Who are the people in favor of the dress code? Who are the people against the dress code? What conclusion might you draw from this list?

   _____

   _____

   _____

2. The article did not specifically state what most parents think about the requirement. How do you think parents feel about it? Why do you think so?

   _____

   _____

   _____

3. The American Civil Liberties Union of Southern California claims that the Long Beach school district's uniform policy is a financial burden on poor families. What arguments might you make both for and against this statement?

   _____

   _____

   _____

• Another Perspective

Uncool in School: The Dress Code Debate

by George Judson
The New York Times

1   No hats, no bare midriffs, no see-through clothing, no underwear showing, no vulgar T-shirts, no sunglasses, no beepers, no cellular phones, no oversized jewelry that can be used as weapons: the more or less
5 standard list of prohibitions that Stamford, Connecticut is considering for its high schools is a world away from dress codes in the '60's, when blue jeans were banned and skirts had to reach the knee.

    But those who are unhappy about the new dress
10 codes—including principals and teachers, as well as students and civil-liberties lawyers—ask whether they are really necessary, or whether they reflect the general unease of adults about the state of education, society and teen-agers.

Reprinted with permission from *The New York Times*, "Uncool in School," George Judson, October 5, 1995.

15   In Stamford, for example, the proposed dress code is
supported by adults like a group of executives who vis-
ited one of the two public high schools and later complained to the district superintendent about students
dressed more for the street corner than the office.

20   "If you haven't been part of big groups of teen-
agers, it can be very overwhelming to walk into a high
school," said Anthony Markosky, the principal of Stamford High School. "And I've got 1,900 teen-agers."

In meetings with school board members, students
25 complained that the board was concerned about image
instead of education. The image Stamford wants to
avoid, in big high schools where wealthy students from
suburban neighborhoods mix with teen-agers from
housing projects and immigrants from dozens of coun-
30 tries, is that of the inner city.

"People don't understand what happens when you
have a corporate culture," said Robert King, a board
member. "It's not enough any more that downtown
Stamford looks good. We want everything to look good,
35 and that includes the schools. We know some people
put their children in other schools because Stamford
schools are supposed to be unsafe." In Stamford High's
cafeteria on a recent day, however, almost no one was
wearing anything except caps that would violate the
40 proposed dress code.

Mr. Markosky says, "I tell the kids, when you get up
in the morning and look in the mirror, ask yourself, 'If
I'm walking down the hall and Mr. Markosky sees me,
what's he going to do?' If you think he's going to send
45 you home, change your clothes."

"I've got eight million things I should be dealing
with, and dress codes are about 84th on my list," he
said. "It's never been a problem."

He stopped to look in on an economics class taught
50 by Joe Carpentieri, who wore a ponytail, a Harley-
Davidson T-Shirt, denim shorts to his knees and deck
shoes without socks.

"He's one of my best teachers," Mr. Markosky said.
"Would he be a different teacher in long pants? I'd take
55 a whole school of people like him."

•Questions for "Uncool in School"

1. Refer to your list of items that should be banned from school. What items in this article would you also ban? Why?

_____

_____

_____

2. Refer to your list of arguments for and against school uniform dress codes. What additional arguments does this article give for and against dress codes? Who is in favor of dress codes? Who is against it? Why?

_____

_____

_____

_____

_____

3. The first article in this chapter appeared in *Education Week*, a newspaper that serves school professionals such as superintendents, school board members, principals, and teachers. The second article appeared in *The New York Times*, a newspaper with a general readership. How does the style of writing reflect the different audiences that these papers serve?

_____

_____

_____

• F. Follow-up Activities

1. Refer to the **Self-Evaluation of Reading Strategies** on pages 60–61. Think about the strategies you used to help yourself understand "Dressing for Success." Check off the strategies you used. Think about the strategies you didn't use, and try to apply them to help yourself understand the readings that follow.

2. Work in groups. Make a list of other people who wear uniforms. What are some reasons that these people wear uniforms? Are they similar to the reasons students might wear uniforms? Why or why not? Compare your list and your reasons with those of the other groups in your class.

3. Work in pairs or groups. You are a committee selected by your school district to determine the dress code for your high school's students. Decide whether you want a uniform or a dress code. Design a uniform or describe dress code requirements that you feel will be acceptable to the school district, the students, and their parents. When you have finished, compare your choice with those of the other groups. As a class, decide which uniform or dress code you will present to the school district for adoption.

4. Work in groups. The school district wants to publicize the new uniform or dress code you have chosen and create a positive public response to it. The school district has asked you to create a slogan and a logo to familiarize the students and parents with the new rule and to help everyone develop a positive attitude towards this new regulation, which will take effect at the beginning of the next school year. When you are finished, as a class, decide which slogan and which logo you will present to the school district for publicity purposes.

• G. Topics for Discussion and Writing

1. Work in groups. Your school district has decided to mandate a dress code for its high school students. Your committee's responsibility is to inform students and their parents of the new code.

   a. Together, compose a letter to the parents informing them of the code. Explain the reasons for the code and how it will benefit both them and their children. Explain the option the parents have to excuse their children from the requirement, and give reasons why they should not do so.
   b. Together, compose a letter to the students informing them of the code. Explain the reasons for the code and how it will benefit them. Try to persuade the students that the dress code will be a positive change for them.

2. As a responsible student, you are not in favor of the uniform dress code. With one or two other students, write a letter to *Education Week*'s editor. Explain why you disagree with the mandatory dress code. Offer alternative suggestions for reducing violence in the schools.

3. **Write in your journal.** During your education, did your schools require uniforms? If so, how did you feel about wearing a uniform in elementary school? In high school? Do you think students in school today feel the same way?

C·H·A·P·T·E·R 2

My Husband, the Outsider

• Prereading Preparation

1. With two or three students, define the term *mixed marriage*. When you are finished, write your definition on the board. Compare yours with the other groups' definitions. As a class, decide what you mean by *mixed marriage*.

Your Group's Definition	The Class's Agreed-on Definition

2. Alone, think about these two questions: What is an American? When is a person an American? Write your responses in your journal, and think about the questions as you read the article.

3. Read the title of the article. What does Marian Hyun mean when she describes her husband as an outsider?

4. Conduct an in-class survey using the questions in the following chart. Record the responses on the chart. You will use your data later when you do an out-of-class survey on the same questions. Discuss your responses in class.

Total # of Respondents: _____

Total # of Men: _____   Total # of Women: _____

Is there a right age to get married?					
Yes		No		Not Sure	
Men	Women	Men	Women	Men	Women
%	%	%	%	%	%
Is it acceptable to marry a person of another race?					
Yes		No		Not Sure	
Men	Women	Men	Women	Men	Women
%	%	%	%	%	%
Should a son or a daughter always marry the person their parents choose?					
Yes		No		Not Sure	
Men	Women	Men	Women	Men	Women
%	%	%	%	%	%
Should a son or a daughter marry a person even if their parents disapprove of the person?					
Yes		No		Not Sure	
Men	Women	Men	Women	Men	Women
%	%	%	%	%	%

My Husband, the Outsider

by Marian Hyun

Newsday

1   When my husband-to-be and I announced our engagement, people were curious about the kind of wedding we would have. He is an Irish-Ukrainian from the Bronx, and a lapsed Catholic, while I am an American-born Korean

5 from New Jersey. Some of my husband's friends must have been expecting an exotic wedding ceremony.

     We disappointed many people. Far from being exotic, or even very religious, our ceremony was performed in English by a Unitarian minister on a hotel balcony. But

10 when my husband and I decided to have 50 guests instead of 150, we caused an uproar among relatives and family friends, especially on the Korean side.

     "It's very embarrassing," my father complained. "Everyone wants to know why you won't listen to me and

15 invite the people you should."

     "Well, whose wedding is this, anyway?" I asked.

     What a dumb question. I had forgotten for a moment that I was dealing with Koreans. It was bad enough that I had decided to marry a non-Korean, but

20 highly insulting that I wasn't giving everyone the chance to snicker over it in person. I found out after the wedding that my father was asked, "How does it feel to have an American son-in-law?"

     "My son-in-law is a good man," he said. "Better to have

25 a good American son-in-law than a bad Korean one."

     He hadn't always felt that way. For years, he ignored the non-Koreans I was dating—it took him about a year to remember my husband's name. But when I was a freshman in college, I dated my father's dream of a son-

30 in-law, David, an American-born Korean from a respected family, who was doing brilliantly at Harvard and had plans for law school. When the relationship ended, my father preferred not to acknowledge the fact.

     When it became clear that David would never be his

35 son-in-law, my father started dropping hints at the dinner table about some handsome and delightful young doctor working for him, who was right off the plane from Seoul—there seemed to be a steady supply. This

Reprinted with permission from Marian Hyun. Excerpt from *Newsday*, March 3, 1991.

started during my senior year in college, and contin-
40 ued until sometime after my engagement.

The one time I did go out with a Korean doctor was
at my mother's request. "Please, just once," she said.
"One of my college friends has a son who wants to get
married, and she thought of you."

45   "You expect me to go out with a guy who lets his
mommy pick his dates?" I asked.

"He's very traditional," she explained. "If you refuse
to meet him, my friend will think I'm too snobby to
want her son in our family. I'll lose face."

50   "OK, just this once," I said reluctantly. A few days
later, I sat in an Indian restaurant with the Korean doctor. After several start-and-stop attempts at conversation, the doctor told me I should live in Korea for a while.

"Korea is a great country," he said. "I think you
55 ought to appreciate it more. And you should learn to
speak Korean. I don't understand why you can't speak
your native language."

"English is my native language," I said. "I wish I could
speak Korean, but I don't have the time to learn it now."

60   "You are Korean," he insisted. "You should speak
your mother tongue." A mouthful of food kept me from
saying more than "Mmmm," but I found myself stab-
bing my tandoori chicken with remarkable violence.

Despite our obvious incompatibility, the doctor
65 kept asking me out. For weeks, I had to turn down invi-
tations to dinner, movies and concerts—even rides to
visit my parents—before he finally stopped calling.

During a visit to Seoul a few years later, I realized
that this kind of dogged persistence during Korean
70 courtship was quite common. In fact, my own father
had used it successfully. My mother told me he proposed to her the day after they were introduced at a
dinner given by matchmaking friends. She told him he
was crazy when she turned him down. Undaunted, he
75 hounded her for three months until she finally gave in.

My parents have now been married for almost 40
years, but what worked for them wasn't about to work
for me. I think one reason my father didn't object to having a non-Korean son-in-law—aside from actually liking
80 my husband—was that he was relieved to have one at all.

When I was 24, he started asking me, "When are you
going to make me a grandfather?"

And when I turned 25, the age when unmarried women in Korea are considered old maids, my other
85 relatives expressed their concern.

"You better hurry up and meet someone," one of my aunts told me. "Do you have a boyfriend?"

"Yes," I said. It was 1990, and I had met my future husband a few months earlier in an office where I was
90 working as a temporary secretary.

"Is he Korean?" she asked.

"No." My aunt considered this for a moment, then said, "You better hurry up and meet someone. Do you want me to help?"

95 My husband saved me from spinsterhood. Just barely, in some eyes—I was married at 26. We received generous gifts, many from people who hadn't been invited to the wedding. This convinced my father more than ever that we should have invited all of his friends
100 and relatives. He felt this way for several years, until one of my sisters got engaged and made elaborate plans to feed and entertain 125 wedding guests.

As the expenses mounted, my father took me aside and asked me to talk to my sister.

"Tell her she should have a small, simple wedding," he said. "Like yours."

• A. Reading Overview: Main Idea, Details, and Summary

Read the passage again. As you read, underline what you think are the most important ideas in the reading. Then, in one or two sentences, write the main idea of the reading. *Use your own words.*

Main idea:

_____

_____

_____

Details:

Use the chart below to list the people the author refers to in the reading. What is each person's opinion of Marian and her marriage? Refer back to the information you underlined in the passage as a guide. When you have finished, write a brief summary of the reading. *Use your own words.*

My Husband, the Outsider

People in the reading	How does this person feel about Marian and the marriage?
Marian	

Summary:

_____

_____

_____

_____

• B. Statement Evaluation

Read the following statements. Then scan the article again quickly to find out if each sentence is **True (T), False (F),** or an **Inference (I).**

1. _____ Marian Hyun's husband is Korean.

2. _____ Marian Hyun's Korean relatives expected a very large wedding.

3. _____ Marian Hyun speaks Korean.

4. _____ Marian Hyun's parents have been married for more than 40 years.

5. _____ If a 25-year-old Korean woman is unmarried, she is an "old maid."

6. _____ Marian Hyun's father will pay for her sister's wedding.

• C. Reading Analysis

Read each question carefully. Either circle the letter or number of the correct answer, or write your answer in the space provided.

1. Read lines 1–6. Why were people curious about the kind of wedding Marian and her husband would have?

    a. because they come from similar backgrounds
    b. because they come from different backgrounds

2. Read lines 9–12. **Caused an uproar** means

    a. The family was very happy
    b. the family was very disturbed
    c. the family all disagreed

3. Read lines 21–25. What is a **son-in-law?**

    _____

4. Read lines 41–49.

    a. **Snobby** means

        1. rich
        2. superior
        3. afraid

    b. **Lose face** means

        1. hurt your face
        2. forget something
        3. become embarrassed

5. Read lines 50–67.

    a. Why was the author **stabbing my tandoori chicken with remarkable violence?**

        1. She didn't like the food.
        2. She wasn't hungry.
        3. She was angry at the Korean doctor.

    b. **Incompatibility** means that Marian and the doctor

        1. did not get along well because they didn't have anything in common
        2. got along well because they had much in common

6. Read lines 68–75.

   a. What is another expression to indicate that Marian's father showed **dogged persistence** in courting Marian's mother?

      _____

   b. These terms mean that Marian's father

      1. was shy about trying to date her mother
      2. pursued her mother insistently
      3. let her mother call him for dates

7. Read lines 98–106. Why does Marian's father ask her to tell her sister **"she should have a small, simple wedding, like yours?"**

   _____

• D. Dictionary Skills

Read the dictionary entry for each word, and consider the context of the sentence from the passge. Write the number of the definition that is appropriate for the context on the line next to the word. Be prepared to explain your choice.

1. When the relationship with David ended, my father preferred not to **acknowledge** the fact.

   acknowledge: _____

   ac·knowl·edge \ik-'nä-iij, ak-\ *vt* **-edged; -edg·ing** [*ac-* (as in *accord*) + *knowledge*] (15c) **1 :** to recognize the rights, authority, or status of **2 :** to disclose knowledge of or agreement with **3 a :** to express gratitude or obligation for   **b :** to take notice of   **c :** to make known the receipt of **4 :** to recognize as genuine or valid ⟨∼ a debt⟩
   syn ACKNOWLEDGE, ADMIT, OWN, AVOW, CONFESS mean to disclose against one's will or inclination. ACKNOWLEDGE implies the disclosing of something that has been or might be concealed ⟨*acknowledged* an earlier peccadillo⟩. ADMIT implies reluctance to disclose, grant, or concede and refers usu. to facts rather than their implications ⟨*admitted* the project was over budget⟩. OWN implies acknowledging something in close relation to oneself ⟨must *own* I know little about computers⟩. AVOW implies boldly declaring, often in the face of hostility, what one might be expected to be silent about ⟨*avowed* that he was a revolutionary⟩. CONFESS may apply to an admission of a weakness, failure, omission, or guilt ⟨*confessed* a weakness for sweets⟩.

2. When I was a freshman in college, I dated my father's **dream** of a son-in-law, David, an American-born Korean from a respected family, who was doing brilliantly at Harvard and had plans for law school.

   dream: _____

   dream \'drēm\ *n, often attrib* [ME *dreem,* fr. OE *drēam* noise, joy, and ON *draumr* dream; akin to OHG *troum* dream] (13c) **1 :** a series of thoughts, images, or emotions occurring during sleep — compare REM SLEEP **2 :** an experience of waking life having the characteristics of a dream: as **a :** a visionary creation of the imagination : DAYDREAM **b :** a state of mind marked by abstraction or release from reality : REVERIE **c :** an object seen in a dreamlike state : VISION **3 :** something notable for its beauty, excellence, or enjoyable quality ⟨the new car is a ∼ to operate⟩ **4 a :** a strongly desired goal or purpose ⟨a ∼ of becoming president⟩ **b :** something that fully satisfies a wish : IDEAL ⟨a meal that was a gourmet's ∼⟩ — **dream·ful** \-fəl\ *adj* — **dream·ful·ly** \-fə-lē\ *adv* — **dream·ful·ness** *n* — **dream·less** *adj* — **dream·less·ly** *adv* — **dream·less·ness** *n* — **dream·like** \'drēm-ˌlīk\ *adj*

3. He is an Irish-Ukrainian from the Bronx, and a lapsed Catholic, while I am an American-born Korean from New Jersey. Some of my husband's friends must have been expecting an **exotic** wedding ceremony.

exotic: _____

ex·ot·ic \ig-'zä-tik\ *adj* [L *exoticus,* fr. Gk *exōtikos,* fr. *exō*] (1599) **1** : introduced from another country : not native to the place where found **2** *archaic* : FOREIGN, ALIEN **3** : strikingly, excitingly, or mysteriously different or unusual **4** : of or relating to striptease 〈~ dancing〉 — **ex·ot·i·cal·ly** \-ti-k(ə-)lē\ *adv* — **ex·ot·ic·ness** \-tik-nəs\ *n*

4. During dinner, the Korean doctor said, "You should learn to speak Korean. I don't understand why you can't speak your native language." "English is my native language," I said. "I wish I could speak Korean, but I don't have the time to learn it now." "You are Korean," he insisted. "You should speak your mother tongue." Despite our obvious **incompatibility**, the doctor kept asking me out.

incompatible: _____

in·com·pat·i·ble \ˌin-kəm-'pa-tə-bəl\ *adj* [ME, fr. MF & ML; MF, fr. ML *incompatibilis,* fr. L *in-* + ML *compatibilis* compatible] (15c) **1** : incapable of being held by one person at one time — used of offices that make conflicting demands on the holder **2** : not compatible: as **a** : incapable of association or harmonious coexistence 〈~ colors〉 **b** : unsuitable for use together because of undesirable chemical or physiological effects 〈~ drugs〉 **c** : not both true 〈~ propositions〉 **d** : incapable of blending into a stable homogeneous mixture — **incompatible** *n* — **in·com·pat·i·bly** \-blē\ *adv*

Pronunciation Guide

\ə\ abut \ᵊ\ kitten, F table \ər\ further \a\ ash \ā\ ace \ä\ mop, mar
\au̇\ out \ch\ chin \e\ bet \ē\ easy \g\ go \i\ hit \ī\ ice \j\ job
\ŋ\ sing \ō\ go \ȯ\ law \ȯi\ boy \th\ thin \t͟h\ the \ü\ loot \u̇\ foot
\y\ yet \zh\ vision \à, k̲, ⁿ, œ, œ̄, ɷe, ɷ̄e, ʸ\

• E. Critical Thinking

Read each question carefully. Write your response in the space provided. Remember there is no one correct answer. Your response depends on what **you** think.

1. Read the first paragraph. Why do you think Marian's husband's family were expecting an exotic wedding ceremony?

   _____

   _____

2. What qualities do you think Marian's father looked for in a possible husband for his daughter?

   _____

   _____

3. What did Marian's mother mean by "losing face"?

   _____

   _____

4. What can you infer about Marian's attitude when she said to her mother, "You expect me to go out with a guy who lets his mommy pick his dates"?

   _____

   _____

5. Reading between the lines, what was Marian's aunt actually saying when she repeated, "You better hurry up and meet someone"?

   _____

   _____

6. Marian talks about her opinion and describes how her mother and father feel. However, she does not discuss her husband's point of view. Why do you think she decided not to write about his opinion?

   _____

   _____

7. What was the author's tone? For example, was she humorous, serious, sarcastic, etc.? What was it that makes you think so?

   _____

   _____

• Another Perspective

Unwelcome in Chinatown
She Looks the Part, But She Doesn't Speak the Language

by Amy Wu
The New York Times

1   When I go to Chinatown for breakfast with my parents or my relatives from Hong Kong, we are ushered
to the best table, offered a variety of special dishes
and treated to warm smiles and solicitous service by
5 the dim sum ladies.
    You might think that because I am Chinese—with the
standard straight hair, yellow skin and slanted eyes—I
would have an inside track in Chinatown. But there are
hundreds of men and women like me in New York who
10 actually get short shrift there because we're ABC's,
American-born Chinese, and we don't speak Cantonese.

Reprinted with permission from *The New York Times*, "Unwelcome in Chinatown," Amy Wu, December 10, 1995.

Whether it's an outdoor market, a stationery store, a bakery or a restaurant, the routine is always the same. ABC's are initially greeted with a smile and a friendly
15 word in Cantonese. Then, when it's discovered that we don't understand, the word, smile and any pretense of friendliness disappear.

It can be embarrassing. One time, a dim sum lady asked me something after she had chatted with my fa-
20 ther. "She doesn't speak Cantonese," my father said. The woman turned scarlet. "What, you never taught her?!" she asked indignantly.

Actually, when I was little, my parents enrolled me in a Saturday morning private school to learn Chinese
25 language and culture. I dropped out when I was 7, after a year or two. I had better things to do on a weekend—mainly to play with my American friends. I wanted nothing more than to be like them, and that's what I became. Now, in Chinatown, I pay the price.
30 Tourists get better treatment than ABC's. Ladies in cheepows bow to them. Waiters fill teapots without being asked. Managers make polite chit-chat, asking how they like Chinatown. Tourists have an excuse for not knowing Cantonese.
35 Well, nobody asked, but I love Chinatown—the smells of fried noodles, the hurly-burly, the feeling of being in another world that is like a little piece of my heritage. I don't think I deserve the treatment I receive there.
40 A Chinatown friend says I should be more understanding. "They live in tiny rooms, in poverty," she said. "They have very little to be proud about except this language no one else understands. You're either in or out."

To them, I'm just another Americanized young per-
45 son, a failure, a traitor. Sure I understand, but most of the time I'm just plain angry. It's not that I want to be accepted, just respected.

Whenever my downtown ABC friends and I want Chinese food without the insults, we go to a take-out
50 place near our New York University dorm. The lo mein is dry and the vegetables are watery, but the cook gives us extra fortune cookies and orange slices and jokes with us in English. He makes us feel at home. Of course, he is an ABC, too.

• Questions for "Unwelcome in Chinatown"

1. Why does Amy Wu feel unwelcome in Chinatown?

   _____

   _____

2. Do you think Amy Wu's experience as an American-born Chinese is a typical experience? Explain your answer.

   _____

   _____

   _____

3. Compare Marian Hyun's experience with that of Amy Wu's. How do you think their upbringing might have been similar? How might it have been different?

   _____

   _____

   _____

4. Apparently neither Marian's parents nor Amy's parents raised their daughters to be bilingual. Why do you think this was so? What do you think about the consequences of Marian and Amy being monolingual? About being so "Americanized"?

   _____

   _____

   _____

• F. Follow-up Activities

1. Refer to the **Self-Evaluation of Reading Strategies** on pages 60–61. Think about the strategies you used to help yourself understand "My Husband, the Outsider." Check off the strategies you used. Think about the strategies you didn't use, and try to apply them to help yourself understand the readings which follow.

2. Alone, or in pairs, interview several people. Use the chart below. When you return to class, compile your data, using the chart on the next page.

Marriage/Nationality Survey

The purpose of this questionnaire is to collect data regarding people's opinions about marriage.

Questions	#1	#2	#3	#4
a. Interviewee is Male/Female (circle one)	M/F	M/F	M/F	M/F
b. Interviewee's age. Are you: under 20? 20–30? 30–40? 40–45? 50+?				
c. What nationality are you?				
1. Is there a "right" age to get married?				
2. If you answered "Yes" to #1, is the right age the same for men and women?				
3. Is it acceptable for someone to marry a person of another race?				
4. Should a son or a daughter always marry the person their parents choose?				
5. Should a son or a daughter marry a person even if their parents disapprove of the person?				

6. What is an American?

   #1. _____

   #2. _____

   #3. _____

   #4. _____

Data Compilation Sheet

Total # of Respondents: _____

Total # of Men: _____   Total # of Women: _____

Is there a "right" age to get married?					
Yes		No		Not Sure	
Men	Women	Men	Women	Men	Women
%	%	%	%	%	%

Is it acceptable to marry a person of another race?					
Yes		No		Not Sure	
Men	Women	Men	Women	Men	Women
%	%	%	%	%	%

Should a son or a daughter always marry the person their parents choose?					
Yes		No		Not Sure	
Men	Women	Men	Women	Men	Women
%	%	%	%	%	%

Should a son or a daughter marry a person even if their parents disapprove of the person?					
Yes		No		Not Sure	
Men	Women	Men	Women	Men	Women
%	%	%	%	%	%

3. a. Refer to your data. What percent of people would probably approve of Marian's decision to marry a non-Korean? Was there a difference in the responses of men and women? If so, what were the differences? Why do you think men and women responded differently?

  b. What are the similarities and differences between your responses as a class and your interviewees' responses? When *is* a person an American? What *is* an American?

4. The following chart shows the percentage of people of various races who got married in the United States **and** who married a person of another race. These statistics cover the years 1970 to 1993. Look at it carefully, then answer the questions that follow.

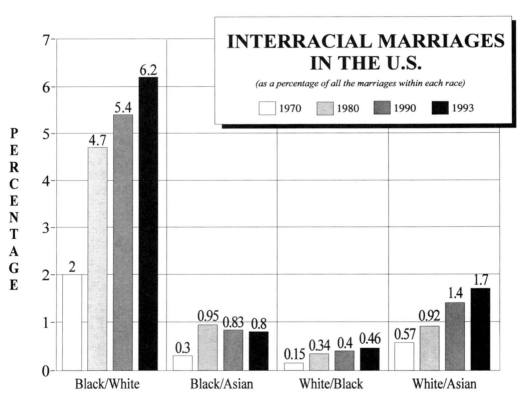

(Race marrying other race)

a. Which race has the highest percentage of interracial marriages?

_____

b. Which rate is higher, the percent of black marriages that involve whites or the percent of white marriages that involve blacks?

_____

c. Which race has the lowest percentage of interracial marriages?

_____

• G. Topics for Discussion and Writing

1. Think about the people in the article "My Husband, the Outsider": Marian, her father, her mother, her dates, her husband. Marian describes how she feels and gives us an idea about how her mother and father feel. How do you think her dates felt? How do you think her husband feels about his new in-laws? How do you think Marian's husband's parents might feel about his marriage?

2. Discuss the conflicts that Marian Hyun had with her family and with her dates. What were some of the causes of these conflicts? For example, were they parent–child disagreements? Were they the result of cultural differences?

3. From this chapter, we know that Marian does not speak Korean, and Amy does not speak Cantonese. Why didn't they learn these languages? Do you think they should be able to speak them? Explain your answer.

4. By yourself, think about your initial answers to these two questions: When is a person an American? What is an American? Do you think any differently after reading the two articles in this chapter? Then, in small groups, discuss your responses. Do you have similar ideas about when a person is an American? About what an American is?

5. **Write in your journal.** Marian did not follow her parents' wish that she marry a Korean man. What is your opinion about her decision?

Beyond Rivalry

Work in your groups to discuss the following questions.

1. How did you get along with your brothers and sisters when you were children? Which sibling did you get along with the best?

2. What kind of relationship do you have now with your brothers and sisters?

3. What do you think happens to the relationship between siblings as they get older? Do they feel closer to each other? Why do you think so?

4. Of the following pairs of siblings, which pair do you think is usually the closest for most people? Why do you think so?

   a. a brother and a sister
   b. two sisters
   c. two brothers

5. Read the title of this article. What aspect of the sibling relationship do you think the writer will focus on?

6. Do an in-class survey of the questions you discussed. When you are finished, compile your data. You will use this information later to compare your responses with the responses of the people you will interview outside the class.

Sibling Survey

Questions	#1	#2	#3	#4
1. How many brothers and sisters do you have?				
2. Where are you in terms of birth order (the oldest, the middle child, the youngest)?				
3. As a child, how well did you get along with your siblings? very well OK not very well badly				
4. Which sibling did you get along with the best?				
5. How do you get along with your siblings today? very well OK not very well badly				
6. Of the following pairs of siblings, which pair do you think is usually the closest? a. a brother and a sister b. two sisters c. two brothers				
7. Which person in your family usually takes responsibility for getting family members together?				

Beyond Rivalry

by Elizabeth Stark
Psychology Today

1   During childhood sisters and brothers are a major part
of each other's lives, for better or for worse. As adults
they may drift apart as they become involved in their own
careers, marriages and families. But in later life, with re-
5   tirement, an empty nest and parents and sometimes
spouses gone, brothers and sisters often turn back to
each other for a special affinity and link to the past.

      "In the stressful, fast-paced world we live in, the
sibling relationship becomes for many the only inti-
10   mate connection that seems to last," says psychologist
Michael Kahn of the University of Hartford. Friends and
neighbors may move away, former coworkers are forgotten, marriages break up, but no matter what, our
sisters and brothers remain our sisters and brothers.

15   This late-life bond may be especially important to the
"Baby Boom" generation[1] now in adulthood, who average
about two or three siblings apiece. High divorce rates
and the decision by many couples to have only one or no
children will force members of this generation to look to
20   their brothers and sisters for support in old age. And, as
psychologist Deborah Gold of the Duke Center for the
Study of Aging and Human Development points out,
"Since people are living longer and are healthier longer,
they will be more capable of giving help."

25   Critical events can bring siblings together or deepen
an existing rift, according to a study by psychologists
Helgola Ross and Joel Milgram of the University of Cincinnati. Parental sickness or death is a prime example.
Ross and Milgram found that siblings immersed in ri-
30   valry and conflict were even more torn apart by the
death or sickness of a parent. Those siblings who had
been close since childhood became closer.

      In a study of older people with sisters and brothers,
Gold found that about 20 percent said they were either
35   hostile or indifferent toward their siblings. Reasons for
the rifts ranged from inheritance disputes to animosity

---

[1] "Baby Boom" generation refers to the people who were born in the United States from 1946 to 1964,
      when the birth rate increased dramatically. Seventeen million children were born during this 18-year
      period.

between spouses. But many of those who had poor relationships felt guilt and remorse. A man who hadn't
spoken with his sister in 20 years described their es-
40 trangement as a "festering sore."

Although most people in Ross and Milgram's study
admitted to some lingering rivalry, it was rarely strong
enough to end the relationship. Only 4 out of the 55
people they interviewed had completely broken with
45 their siblings and only 1 of the 4 felt comfortable with
the break, leaving the researchers to ask, "Is it psycho-
logically impossible to disassociate oneself from one's
siblings in the way one can forget old friends or even
former mates?"

50 As brothers and sisters advance into old age "closeness increases and rivalry diminishes," explains Victor
Cicirelli, a psychologist at Purdue University. Most of
the elderly people he interviewed said they had sup-
portive and friendly dealings and got along well or
55 very well with their brothers and sisters. Only 4 percent got along poorly.

Gold found that as people age they often become
more involved with and interested in their siblings.
Fifty-three percent of those she interviewed said that
60 contact with their sisters and brothers increased in late
adulthood. With family and career obligations reduced,
many said they had more time for each other. Others
said that they felt it was "time to heal wounds." A man
who had recently reconciled with his brother told Gold,
65 "There's something that lets older people put aside the
bad deeds of the past and focus a little on what we
need now . . . especially when it's brothers and sisters."

Another reason for increased contact was anxiety
about a sister's or brother's declining health. Many
70 would call more often to "check in" and see how the
other was doing. Men, especially, reported feeling increased responsibility for a sibling; women were more
likely to cite emotional motivations such as feelings of
empathy and security.

75 Siblings also assume special importance as other
sources of contact and support dwindle. Each of us
moves through life with a "convoy" of people who supply comfort and nurturance, says psychologist Toni C.
Antonucci of the University of Michigan. As we age, the
80 size of the convoy gradually declines because of death,
sickness or moving. "Brothers and sisters who may not

have been important convoy members earlier in life can become so in old age," Gold says. And they do more than fill in gaps. Many people told Gold that the loneli-
85 ness they felt could not be satisfied by just anyone. They wanted a specific type of relationship, one that only someone who had shared their past could provide.

This far-reaching link to the past is a powerful bond between siblings in later life. "There's a review process
90 we all go through in old age to resolve whether we are pleased with our lives," Gold explains. "A sibling can help retrieve a memory and validate our experiences. People have said to me, 'I can remember some with my spouse or with friends. But the only person who goes
95 all the way back is my sister or brother.'"

Cicirelli agrees that reviewing the past together is a rewarding activity. "Siblings have a very important role in maintaining a connection to early life," he says. "Discussing the past evokes the warmth of early family life.
100 It validates and clarifies events of the early years." Furthermore, he has found that encouraging depressed older people to reminisce with a sister or brother can improve their morale.

Some of the factors that affect how much contact sib-
105 lings will have, such as how near they live, are obvious. Others are more unexpected—for example, whether there is a sister in the clan. Cicirelli found that elderly people most often feel closest to a sister and are more likely to keep in touch through her. According to Gold, sisters, by
110 tradition, often assume a caretaking and kin-keeping role, especially after the death of their mother. "In many situations you see two brothers who don't talk to each other that much but keep track of each other through their sisters," she says. Researchers have found that the
115 bond between sisters is strongest, followed by the one between sisters and brothers and, last, between brothers.

Sisters and brothers who live near each other will, as a matter of course, see more of each other. But Cicirelli says that proximity is not crucial to a strong
120 relationship later in life. "Because of multiple chronic illnesses, people in their 80s and 90s can't get together that easily. Even so, the sibling seems to evoke positive feelings based on the images or feelings inside."

Gold's findings support this assertion. During a
125 two-year period, contact among her respondents decreased slightly, but positive feelings increased. "Just

the idea that the sibling is alive, that 'there is someone I can call,' is comforting."

Although older people may find solace in the thought that their siblings are there if they need them, rarely do they call each other for help or offer each other instrumental support, such as loaning money, running errands or performing favors. "Even though you find siblings saying that they'd be glad to help each other and saying they would ask for help if necessary, rarely do they ask," Cicirelli points out.

Gold believes that there are several reasons siblings don't turn to each other more for instrumental help. First, since they are usually about the same age, they may be equally needy or frail. Another reason is that many people consider their siblings safety nets who will save them after everything else has failed. A son or daughter will almost always be turned to first. It's more acceptable in our society to look up or down the family ladder for help than sideways.

Finally, siblings may not turn to each other for help because of latent rivalry. They may believe that if they need to call on a brother or sister they are admitting that the other person is a success and "I am a failure." Almost all of the people in Gold's study said they would rather continue on their own than ask their sister or brother for help. But she found that a crisis beyond control would inspire "a 'rallying' of some or all siblings around the brother or sister in need."

Despite the quarreling and competition many people associate with the mere mention of their sisters and brothers, most of us, Gold says, will find "unexpected strengths in this relationship in later life."

• A. Reading Overview: Main Idea, Details, and Summary

Read the passage again. As you read, underline what you think are the most important ideas in the reading. Then, in one or two sentences, write the main idea of the reading. *Use your own words.*

Main idea:

_____

_____

_____

Details:

Use the outline below to organize the information about siblings' relationships. Refer back to the information you underlined in the passage as a guide. When you have finished, write a brief summary of the reading. *Use your own words.*

Beyond Rivalry

  I. Social Connections

    A.

        1. have careers

        2.

        3.

    B. Older Adult Siblings

        1.

        2.

        3.

 II. Effects of Critical Events in Siblings' Lives

    A.

    B.

III.

    A.

    B.

    C. 53 percent increased contact

        1.

        2. anxiety about sibling's health

        3.

        4. need link to the past

IV.

    A. proximity

    B.

V. Factors Affecting Why Siblings Don't Ask Each Other for Help

    A.

    B.

    C.

Summary:

_____

_____

_____

_____

• B. Statement Evaluation

Read the following statements. Then scan the article again quickly to find out if each sentence is **True (T), False (F),** or **Not Mentioned (NM)** in the article.

1. _____ Critical events always bring siblings closer together.

2. _____ Most older people are angry or hostile towards their siblings.

3. _____ Almost all brothers and sisters have more contact with each other as they age.

4. _____ Older male siblings argue more than older female siblings do.

5. _____ Older brothers and sisters enjoy talking together about the past.

6. _____ The age difference between siblings is an important factor in sibling rivalry.

7. _____ Older people prefer to call their siblings for help instead of their children.

• C. Reading Analysis

Read each question carefully. Either circle the letter or number of the correct answer, or write your answer in the space provided.

1. Read lines 25–32.

   a. **"Critical events can bring siblings together or deepen an existing rift."** This sentence means that critical events
      1. can have opposite effects on siblings
      2. always make siblings feel closer
      3. always pull siblings apart

   b. What are examples of **critical events** in the paragraph?
   _____

2. Read lines 33–40.

   a. What is an **estrangement?**
      1. a family
      2. a closeness
      3. a separation

   b. How do you know?
   _____

3. Read lines 41–49. Why did the researchers ask this question?

   a. The majority of the people in the study did not have contact with their siblings. Researchers wonder why.
   b. The majority of the people in the study had contact with their siblings. Researchers wonder why.

4. Read lines 50–56. The authors states that "closeness increases and rivalry diminishes." **Diminishes** is

   a. a synonym of **increases**
   b. an antonym of **increases**

5. Read lines 75–87.

   a. Which word in this paragraph is a synonym of **dwindle?**
   _____

   b. What is a **convoy** of people?
   _____

c. **"Brothers and sisters who may not have been important convoy members earlier in life can become so in old age."** In this sentence, **so** means

   1. siblings can become important convoy members
   2. as a result
   3. very

6. Read lines 88–95. What is the meaning of **all the way back?**

   _____

7. Read lines 104–116.

  a. What is the meaning of **clan?**
    1. family
    2. old people
    3. hospital

  b. What is the meaning of **kin?**
    1. health
    2. communication
    3. relatives

8. Read lines 117–123. What word in this paragraph is a synonym of the phrase **live near each other?**

   _____

9. Read lines 124–136.

  a. What does **solace** mean?
    1. sibling
    2. comfort
    3. anger

  b. What are examples of **instrumental support?**

   _____

  c. How do you know?

   _____

• D. Dictionary Skills

Read the entry for each word, and consider the context of the sentence from the passage. Write the number of the definition that is appropriate for the context on the line next to the word. Be prepared to explain your choice.

1. The late-life **bond** between brothers and sisters may be especially important to the "Baby Boom" generation now in adulthood.

   Brothers and sisters who may not have been important convoy members earlier in life can become so in old age. Many people said that the loneliness they felt could not be satisfied by just anyone. They wanted a specific type of relationship, one that only someone who had shared their past could provide. This far-reaching link to the past is a powerful **bond** between siblings in later life.

bond: _____

bond \'bänd\ *n* [ME *band, bond* — more at BAND] (12c)   **1** : something that binds or restrains : FETTER   **2** : a binding agreement : COVENANT   **3 a** : a band or cord used to tie something   **b** : a material or device for binding   **c** : an attractive force that holds together the atoms, ions, or groups of atoms in a molecule or crystal   **d** : an adhesive, cementing material, or fusible ingredient that combines, unites, or strengthens   **4** : a uniting or binding element or force : TIE ⟨the ~s of friendship⟩   **5 a** : an obligation made binding by a money forfeit; *also* : the amount of the money guarantee   **b** : one who acts as bail or surety   **c** : an interest-bearing certificate of public or private indebtedness   **d** : an insurance agreement pledging surety for financial loss caused to another by the act or default of a third person or by some contingency over which the third person may have no control   **6** : the systematic lapping of brick in a wall   **7** : the state of goods made, stored, or transported under the care of bonded agencies until the duties or taxes on them are paid   **8** : a 100-proof straight whiskey aged at least four years under government supervision before being bottled — called also *bonded whiskey*   **9** : BOND PAPER

2. A sibling can help retrieve a memory and validate our experiences. Discussing the past can **evoke** the warmth of early family life.

   Because of multiple chronic illnesses, people in their 80s and 90s can't get together that easily. Even so, the sibling seems to **evoke** positive feelings based on the images or feelings inside.

evoke: _____

evoke \i-'vōk\ *vt* evoked; evok·ing [F *évoquer*, fr. L *evocare*, fr. e- + *vocare* to call — more at VOCATION] (ca. 1626)   **1** : to call forth or up: as   **a** : CONJURE 2a ⟨~ evil spirits⟩   **b** : to cite esp. with approval or for support : INVOKE   **c** : to bring to mind or recollection ⟨this place ~s memories⟩   **2** : to recreate imaginatively   *syn* see EDUCE

3. The sibling relationship becomes for many the only intimate connection that seems to **last.** Friends and neighbors may move away, former coworkers are forgotten, marriages break up, but our brothers and sisters remain our brothers and sisters.

last: _____

last \\'last\\ *vb* [ME, fr. OE *lǣstan* to last, follow; akin to OE *lāst* footprint] *vi* (bef. 12c) **1 :** to continue in time   **2 a :** to remain fresh or unimpaired : ENDURE   **b :** to manage to continue (as in a course of action)   **c :** to continue to live ∼ *vt* **1 :** to continue in existence or action as long as or longer than — often used with *out* ⟨couldn't ∼ out the training program⟩   **2 :** to be enough for the needs of ⟨the supplies will ∼ them a week⟩   *syn* see CONTINUE — **last·er** *n*

4. A sibling can help retrieve a memory and **validate** our experiences. Siblings have a very important role in maintaining a connection to early life. Discussing the past evokes the warmth of early family life. It **validates** and clarifies events of the early years.

validate: _____

val·i·date \\'va-lə-ˌdāt\\ *vt* **-dat·ed; -dat·ing** (1648) **1 a :** to make legally valid   **b :** to grant official sanction to by marking   **c :** to confirm the validity of (an election); *also :* to declare (a person) elected   **2 :** to support or corroborate on a sound or authoritative basis ⟨experiments designed to ∼ the hypothesis⟩   *syn* see CONFIRM

Pronunciation Guide

\\ə\\ **abut**   \\ʰ\\ **kitten, F table**   \\ər\\ **further**   \\a\\ **ash**   \\ā\\ **ace**   \\ä\\ **mop, mar**
\\au̇\\ **out**   \\ch\\ **chin**   \\e\\ **bet**   \\ē\\ **easy**   \\g\\ **go**   \\i\\ **hit**   \\ī\\ **ice**   \\j\\ **job**
\\ŋ\\ **sing**   \\ō\\ **go**   \\ȯ\\ **law**   \\ȯi\\ **boy**   \\th\\ **thin**   \\t̲h̲\\ **the**   \\ü\\ **loot**   \\u̇\\ **foot**
\\y\\ **yet**   \\zh\\ **vision**   \\à, k̲, ⁿ, œ, œ̄, ue, ūe, ʸ\\

• E. Critical Thinking

Read each question carefully. Write your response in the space provided. Remember that there is no one correct answer. Your response depends on what **you** think.

1. Why might the "Baby Boom" generation have a high divorce rate? Why might this group have fewer children than previous American generations?

   _____
   _____
   _____

2. Is there a difference between men's and women's feelings toward their siblings? Explain your answer.

   _____
   _____
   _____

3. Why do sisters often assume a caretaking role, especially after the death of their mother?

   _____
   _____
   _____

4. Why did contact among siblings decrease, while positive feelings among them increased?

   _____
   _____
   _____

• Another Perspective

Blended Family Birth Order: How Middles Seek Respect in the Step-Family

by Dr. Kevin Leman

(excerpt from *Living in a Step-Family without Getting Stepped on*)

 Middle-born children will tell you that they usually didn't feel all that special while growing up. The first-
1 born had his spot—carrier of the family banner and re-sponsible for everything. The last born had his comfy little role, but the middle born had no distinctive place to call his own . . .
5 Middle-borns just seem to be easily overlooked, and maybe that's why there are so few pictures of them in the family photo album. There may be hundreds, seem-ingly thousands, of pictures of the firstborn. And the baby of the family will make sure she attracts enough at-
10 tention to fill a few album pages. For some strange rea-son, however, which I have confirmed by polling

middle-born children around the world, there are seldom
15 many pictures of the middle child, and what photos
there are have him included with the others—squeezed
again between the older sibling and the younger sibling.

Another thing that can be said of many middle
born children is that they typically place great impor-
20 tance on their peer group. The middle child is well-
known for going outside the home to make friends
faster than anybody else in the family. When a child
feels like a fifth wheel at home, friends become very
important; as a result, many middle children (but not
25 all, of course) tend to be the social lions of the family.
While firstborns, typically, have fewer friends, middle
children often have many.

Middle children have a propensity to leave home first
and live farther away from the family than anyone else. I
30 observed a dramatic illustration of this tendency while I
was a guest on Oprah Winfrey's show. The subject that
day was sibling rivalry. Three charming young women, all
sisters, were among the guests, and we quickly learned
that the firstborn and the last born were residents of the
35 Eastern state where they had grown up. They had settled
down near their parents and other family members. But
the middle child had moved to the West Coast.

I suppose she could have gotten another two thousand miles farther away by moving to Hawaii, but her
40 point was still well made. Middle children are the ones
who will most often physically distance themselves
from the rest of the family. It's not necessarily because
they're on the outs with everyone else. They simply
like to do their own thing, make their own friends, and
45 live their own lives . . .

All of this is not to say that middle children totally ignore their siblings or the rest of the family. One common
characteristic of the middle child is that she is a good
mediator or negotiator. She comes naturally into this role
50 because she's often right in the middle, between big
brother and little sister, whatever the case may be. And
because she can't have Mom and Dad all to herself, she
learns the fine art of compromise. Obviously, these skills
are assets in adult life, and middle children often become
55 the best adjusted adults in the family.

• Questions for Another Perspective

1. List some of the personality traits and behaviors that Dr. Leman attributes to middle children.

   _____

   _____

   _____

2. How do you think these traits and behaviors might affect the middle child's relationship with his/her siblings during childhood?

   _____

   _____

   _____

3. How do you think these traits and behavior might affect the middle child's relationship with his/her siblings later on in life?

   _____

   _____

   _____

• F. Follow-up Activities

1. Refer to the **Self-Evaluation of Reading Strategies** on the next page. Think about the strategies you used to help yourself understand "Beyond Rivalry." Check off the strategies you used. Evaluate your strategy use over the first three chapters. Which strategies have you begun to use that you didn't use in the first or second chapter? Which strategies do you use consistently? Which additional strategies do you use that you have added to the list? To what extent have you applied these strategies to other reading you do?

Self-Evaluation of Reading Strategies

Strategies	Readings		
	"Dressing for Success"	"My Husband, the Outsider"	"Beyond Rivalry"
I read the title and try to predict what the reading will be about.			
I use my knowledge of the world to help me understand the text.			
I read as though I *expect* the text to have meaning.			
I use illustrations to help me understand the text.			
I ask myself questions about the text.			
I use a variety of types of context clues.			
I take chances in order to identify meaning.			
I continue if I am not successful.			
I identify and underline main ideas.			
I connect details with main ideas.			
I summarize the reading in my own words.			
I skip unnecessary words.			
I look up words correctly in the dictionary.			
I connect the reading to other material I have read.			
I do not translate into my native language.			

2. Alone, or in pairs, interview several people outside class. When you return to class, compile your data. What are the similarities and differences between your responses as a class and your interviewees' responses?

Sibling Survey

The purpose of this questionnaire is to collect data regarding people and their siblings. Interview people with at least one sibling.

	1	#2	#3	#4
Interviewee's gender	M/F	M/F	M/F	M/F
Questions				
1. How many brothers and sisters do you have?				
2. Where are you in terms of birth order (oldest, middle child, youngest)?				
3. As a child, how well did you get along with your siblings? very well OK not very well badly				
4. Which sibling did you get along with the best?				
5. How do you get along with your siblings today? very well OK not very well badly				
6. Of the following pairs of siblings, which pair do you think is usually the closest? a. a brother and a sister b. two sisters c. two brothers				
7. Which person in your family usually takes responsibility for getting family members together?				

• G. Topics for Discussion and Writing

1. Write a composition about one of your siblings. What was your relationship like? Why did you feel this way about each other? How is your relationship today? If you are an only child, write about whether you would have preferred to have siblings. Explain your preference.

2. Do you think it is important for children to have brothers and sisters? If so, how many? Do you think that only children may be at a disadvantage when they get older? Why or why not? Discuss this issue with your classmates.

3. In your opinion, how important is the bond between siblings? How does this bond change as siblings get older? Give examples from your own life. When you need help, who do you turn to? Why?

4. What is your birth order? Do you think your role is your family has been influenced by your position? If so, in what ways? Write a composition.

5. **Write in your journal.** Which member of your family assumes the kin-keeping role described in this article? Why?

Unit I Review

• H. Crossword Puzzle

• **Crossword Puzzle Clues**

Across

1. unusual; excitingly different
4. support against opposition
5. family
9. unable to get along with because of differences
12. cure
13. verbal or written support
14. ideal
19. recognize; take notice of
20. confirm; verify
22. a tie; a uniting force
23. brother or sister
24. "read between the lines"
26. a suit or action in law

Down

1. bring to mind; call forth a memory
2. a choice
3. relatives
6. endure; remain unimpaired
7. initiate; set in motion
8. a disagreement, especially one with two opposing viewpoints
10. separation
11. promise or commitment to marry
14. dwindle; decrease
15. American-born Chinese
16. required
17. marriage ceremony
18. able to speak two languages fluently
21. comfort
25. break

Influences on Our Lives: Nature Versus Nurture

Who Lives Longer?

• Prereading Preparation

1. In groups of three or four, speculate on how long the average person lives. Discuss factors that affect a person's longevity, both positively and negatively. For example, diet is a factor. What you eat may positively or negatively affect your longevity. Use the chart below to help you organize your ideas.

FACTORS	Positive	Negative

2. After you have organized the factors, prepare a brief (two or three minute) report that one of you will present to the class.

3. After all the groups in the class have presented their views, work in your group again. Review your chart; make any revisions you want, and then report your group's factors to the class.

4. Read the title of this article. Who do you think the article will say lives longer?

Who Lives Longer?

by Patricia Skalka
McCall's

1   How to live longer is a topic that has fascinated mankind for centuries. Today scientists are beginning to separate the facts from the fallacies surrounding the aging process. Why is it that some people reach a ripe

5   old age and others do not? Several factors influencing longevity are set at birth, but surprisingly, many others are elements that can be changed. Here is what you should know.

Some researchers divide the elements determining

10   who will live longer into two categories: fixed factors and changeable factors. Gender, race and heredity are fixed factors—they can't be reversed, although certain long-term social changes can influence them. For example, women live longer than men—at birth, their life

15   expectancy is about seven to eight years more. However, cigarette smoking, drinking and reckless driving could shorten this advantage.

There is increasing evidence that length of life is also influenced by a number of elements that are

20   within your ability to control. The most obvious are physical life-style factors.

Health Measures

According to a landmark study of nearly 7,000

25   adults in Alameda County, California, women can add up to seven years to their lives and men 11 to 12 years by following seven simple health practices: (1) Don't smoke. (2) If you drink, do so only moderately. (3) Eat breakfast regularly. (4) Don't eat between meals. (5)

30   Maintain normal weight. (6) Sleep about eight hours a night. (7) Exercise moderately.

Cutting calories may be the single most significant life-style change you can make. Experiments have shown that in laboratory animals, a 40 percent calorie

35   reduction leads to a 50 percent extension in longevity. "Eating less has a more profound and diversified effect on the aging process than does any other life-style change," Says Byung P. Yu, Ph.D., professor of physiology at the University of Texas Health Science Center at

40 San Antonio. "It is the only factor we know of in laboratory animals that is an anti-aging factor."

Psychosocial Factors

A long life, however, is not just the result of being
45 good to your body and staving off disease. All the various factors that constitute and influence daily life can
be critical too. In searching for the ingredients to a
long, healthy existence, scientists are studying links
between longevity and the psychological and social as-
50 pects of human existence. The following can play significant roles in determining your longevity:

Social integration

Researchers have found that people who are socially
55 integrated—they are part of a family network, are married, participate in structured group activities—live
longer.

Early studies indicated that the more friends and
relatives you had, the longer you lived. Newer studies
60 focus on the types of relationships that are most beneficial. "Larger networks don't always seem to be ad-
vantageous to women," says epidemiologist Teresa
Seeman, Ph.D., associate research scientist at Yale University. "Certain kinds of ties add more demands
65 rather than generate more help."

Autonomy

A feeling of autonomy or control can come from
having a say in important decisions (where you live,
70 how you spend your money) or from being surrounded
by people who inspire confidence in your ability to
master certain tasks (yes, you can quit smoking, you
will get well). Studies show these feelings bring a sense
of well-being and satisfaction with life. "Autonomy is a
75 key factor in successful aging," says Toni Antonucci,
associate research scientist at the Institute for Social
Research at the University of Michigan.

Stress and Job Satisfaction

80 Researchers disagree on how these factors affect longevity. There isn't enough data available to support a
link between stress and longevity, says Edward L.
Schneider, M.D., dean of the Andrus Gerontology Center

at the University of Southern California. Animal re-
85 search, however, provides exciting insights. In studies
with laboratory rats, certain types of stress damage the
immune system and destroy brain cells, especially those
involved in memory. Other kinds of stress enhance immune function by 20 to 30 percent, supporting a theory
90 first advanced by Hans Selye, M.D., Ph.D., a pioneer in
stress research. He proposed that an exciting, active and
meaningful life contributes to good health.

The relationship between job satisfaction and longevity also remains in question. According to some re-
95 searchers, a satisfying job adds years to a man's life,
while volunteer work increases a woman's longevity.
These findings may change as more women participate
in the work force. One study found that clerical workers suffered twice as many heart attacks as homemak-
100 ers. Factors associated with the coronary problems
were suppressed hostility, having a nonsupportive
boss, and decreased job mobility.

Environment
105   Where you live can make a difference in how long you
live. A study by the California Department of Health Services in Berkeley found a 40 percent higher mortality rate
among people living in a poverty area compared to those
in a nonpoverty area. "The difference was not due to age,
110 sex, health care or life-style," says George A. Kaplan,
Ph.D., chief of the department's Human Population Laboratory. The resulting hypothesis: A locale can have environmental characteristics, such as polluted air or water,
or socioeconomic characteristics, such as a high crime
115 rate and level of stress, that make it unhealthy.

Socioeconomic Status
People with higher incomes, more education and
high-status occupations tend to live longer. Research-
120 ers used to think this was due to better living and job
conditions, nutrition and access to health care, but
these theories have not held up. Nevertheless, the differences can be dramatic. Among women 65 to 74
years old, those with less than an eighth-grade educa-
125 tion are much more likely to die than are women who
have completed at least one year of college.

What You Can Do

The message from the experts is clear. There are many ways to add years to your life. Instituting sound
130 health practices and expanding your circle of acquaintances and activities will have a beneficial effect. The good news about aging, observes Erdman B. Palmore of the Center for the Study of Aging and Human Development at Duke Medical Center in North Carolina, is many
135 of the factors related to longevity are also related to life satisfaction.

• A. Reading Overview: Main Idea, Details, and Summary

Read the passage again. As you read, underline what you think are the most important ideas in the reading. Then, in one or two sentences, write the main idea of the reading. *Use your own words.*

Main idea:

_____

_____

_____

Details:

Complete the chart below to organize the information in the article. Refer back to the information you underlined in the passage as a guide. When you have finished, write a brief summary of the reading. *Use your own words.*

Who Lives Longer?

_____	Changeable Factors	
	_____	_____
A. gender	1.	1.
B.	2.	2.
C.	3.	3.
	4.	4.
	5.	5.
	6.	
	7.	

What you can do:

A.

B.

Summary:

_____

_____

_____

_____

• B. Statement Evaluation

Read the following statements. Then scan the article again quickly to find out if each sentence is **True (T), False (F),** or **Not Mentioned (NM)** in the article.

1. _____ There is nothing you can do to increase longevity.

2. _____ Laboratory rats that exercised lived longer than those that did not exercise.

3. _____ Eating less may help you live longer.

4. _____ There may be a connection between longevity and psychological factors.

5. _____ Women who work outside the home have more heart attacks than working men do.

6. _____ People who live in poverty areas live longer than people who live in nonpoverty areas.

7. _____ People with higher socioeconomic status tend to live longer than those with lower socioeconomic status.

• C. Reading Analysis

Read each question carefully. Either circle the letter or number of the correct answer, or write your answer in the space provided.

1. a. Read lines 1–4. Which word means the opposite of **fact?**

    _____

    b. How do you know?

    _____

2. Read lines 4–7. People who **"reach a ripe old age"** are people who

    a. die young
    b. are women
    c. live a long time

3. Read lines 9–17. **Fixed factors** are those that

    a. we can change
    b. we are born with
    c. can be reversed

4. In lines 12, 14, and 55, what follows the dashes (—)?

    a. explanations
    b. causes
    c. new ideas

5. Read lines 11–17. What are examples of **certain long-term social changes?**

    _____

6. Read line 28. **"If you drink, do so only moderately."** What does this sentence mean?

    a. Do not drink.
    b. Drink as much as you want.
    c. Only drink a little.

7. Read lines 50–51. What does **the following** refer to?

    _____

8. Read lines 68–73. **Having a say** means

    a. having an opinion
    b. having a choice
    c. speaking loudly

9. Read lines 80–81. What do **these factors** refer to?

_____

10. Read lines 98–102. **Coronary problems** are

    a. hostility
    b. dissatisfaction with your job
    c. heart attacks

11. Read lines 105–115. What is a **hypothesis?**

    a. a theory
    b. a fact
    c. a law

• D. Dictionary Skills

Read the entry for each word, and consider the context of the sentence from the passage. Write the number of the definition that is appropriate for the context on the line next to the word. Be prepared to explain your choice.

1. The study of nearly 7,000 adults in California was a **landmark** in the field of health. According to the study, women can add up to seven years to their lives and men 11 to 12 years by following seven simple health practices.

   landmark: _____

   land·mark \-ₘärk\ *n* (bef. 12c) **1 :** an object (as a stone or tree) that marks the boundary of land **2 a :** a conspicuous object on land that marks a locality   **b :** an anatomical structure used as a point of orientation in locating other structures   **3 :** an event or development that marks a turning point or a stage   **4 :** a structure (as a building) of unusual historical and usu. aesthetic interest; *esp :* one that is officially designated and set aside for preservation

2. Eating less has a more **profound** effect on the aging process than does any other lifestyle change. It is the only factor we know of in laboratory animals that is an anti-aging factor.

   profound: _____

   pro·found \prə-'faùnd, prō-\ *adj* [ME, fr. MF *profond* deep, fr. L *profundus,* fr. *pro-* before + *fundus* bottom — more at PRO-, BOTTOM] (14c) **1 a :** having intellectual depth and insight   **b :** difficult to fathom or understand   **2 a :** extending far below the surface   **b :** coming from, reaching to, or situated at a depth : DEEP-SEATED ⟨a ~ sigh⟩   **3 a** : characterized by intensity of feeling or quality   **b :** all encompassing : COMPLETE ⟨~ sleep⟩ — **pro·found·ly** \-'faùn(d)-lē\ *adv* — **pro·found·ness** \-'faùn(d)-nəs\ *n*

3. A feeling of autonomy or control can come from having a **say** in important decisions (where you live, how you spend your money).

   say: _____

   say *n, pl* **says** \'sāz, *Southern also* 'sez\ (1571) **1** *archaic :* something that is said : STATEMENT   **2 :** an expression of opinion ⟨had my ~⟩   **3** : a right or power to influence action or decision; *esp :* the authority to make final decisions

Pronunciation Guide

\ə\ abut   \ᵊ\ kitten, F table   \ər\ further   \a\ ash   \ā\ ace   \ä\ mop, mar
\aù\ out   \ch\ chin   \e\ bet   \ē\ easy   \g\ go   \i\ hit   \ī\ ice   \j\ job
\ŋ\ sing   \ō\ go   \ò\ law   \òi\ boy   \th\ thin   \th\ the   \ü\ loot   \ù\ foot
\y\ yet   \zh\ vision   \ā, k̲, ⁿ, œ, œ̄, ue, ūe, ᵊ\

4. Instituting **sound** health practices and expanding your circle of acquaintances and activities will have a beneficial effect.

sound: _____

sound \\'saȯnd\\ *adj* [ME, fr. OE *gesund;* akin to OHG *gisunt* healthy] (13c) **1 a :** free from injury or disease : exhibiting normal health **b** : free from flaw, defect, or decay ⟨~ timber⟩ **2 :** SOLID, FIRM; *also* : STABLE **3 a :** free from error, fallacy, or misapprehension ⟨~ reasoning⟩ **b :** exhibiting or based on thorough knowledge and experience ⟨~ scholarship⟩ **c :** legally valid ⟨a ~ title⟩ **d :** logically valid and having true premises **e :** agreeing with accepted views : ORTHODOX **4 a :** THOROUGH **b :** deep and undisturbed ⟨a ~ sleep⟩ **c** : HARD, SEVERE ⟨a ~ whipping⟩ **5 :** showing good judgment or sense *syn* see HEALTHY, VALID — **sound·ly** \\'saȯn(d)-lē\\ *adv* — **sound·ness** \\'saȯn(d)-nəs\\ *n*

• E. Critical Thinking

Read each question carefully. Write your response in the space provided. Remember that there is no one correct answer. Your response depends on what **you** think.

1. What tone does the author set at the end of the article? Is she upbeat, pessimistic, matter-of-fact, etc.?

   _____

   _____

2. Does the author of "Who Lives Longer?" believe that increasing life expectancy is a desirable goal? Explain your answer.

   _____

   _____

3. Why does eating have such a dramatic positive effect on longevity?

   _____

   _____

4. Why do you think volunteer work increases a woman's longevity?

   _____

   _____

5. How are clerical workers and homemakers similar? Why do you think clerical workers suffer twice as many heart attacks as homemakers?

   _____

   _____

• **Another Perspective**

More Senior Citizens, Fewer Kids

by Jessie Cheng
Free China Review

1   "Thirty years from now, it will be rare to see children walking along the streets of Taiwan," says Chen Kuan-jeng, a research fellow in the Institute of Sociology at Academia Sinica. "Instead, the streets will be full of eld-
5 erly people." Chen's prediction may sound a bit drastic, but he voices a growing concern among sociologists over the dramatic shift under way in Taiwan society toward a graying population. As in many developed countries, island families are having fewer children, while at
10 the same time the average life span is increasing to create a larger and larger pool of senior citizens.

Between 1953 and 1993, the annual birthrate declined from about forty-five births per thousand persons to less than sixteen. During the same period, the
15 average number of children per Taiwan couple declined by more than two-thirds, from 7 to 1.7. The current average is below that of the United States (2
children per couple), mainland China (1.9), and Britain
or France (both 1.8). The Taiwan figure also means that
20 since 1984 the birthrate has dropped below the "re-
placement level." Sociologists predict that within forty
years, the total population will be declining.

Another trend is also changing the face of Taiwan's
population: the average life span is steadily rising, lead-
25 ing to a growing proportion of elderly people. In 1951,
local men lived an average of 53 years, and women lived
56 years. Today, men average 72 years and women 77.
Because the trend toward fewer children and more senior
citizens is expected to continue, sociologists predict that
30 the elderly proportion of the population will increase
steadily. While persons aged over 65 made up just over 7
percent of the population in 1994, they are expected to
account for 22 percent by the year 2036—a figure that
could mean more than five million senior citizens.

35 The result is an overall "graying" of society and a
new set of social welfare needs that must be met—nursing homes rather than nursery schools, day care programs for the elderly rather than for preschoolers.
Social scientists predict these demands will be hard to
40 fulfill. "In the future, there won't be enough young
people to support the older people," says Chen. Sociologists are particularly concerned that expanding health
care costs for senior citizens will mean a large financial
burden for taxpayers. Another concern is that a dwin-
45 dling population of working-age adults will slow economic growth.

Patterns in Taiwan's population growth looked far
different just a generation ago. During the 1950s, the
island's population zoomed from 7.6 million to a 1960
50 figure of 10.8 million. The centuries-old belief that
more children bring luck to a family was strong among
local residents.

But as the decade came to a close, the rapid population increase began to alarm sociologists. Opposition
55 notwithstanding, the government launched a pre-preg-
nancy health campaign in 1959 which included teach-

ing birth control methods through public hospitals and
health stations (community out-patient clinics). Still,
Taiwan's population grew from 14.7 million to 17.8
60 million during the 1970s, and social scientists continued to urge further population control measures.

The 1980s marked a turning point in population control. In addition to official family planning campaigns, a
number of social factors have led to the declining birth-
65 rate. For example, couples are marrying later, and a growing number of young people are opting to stay single.

But sociologists worry that population control measures have gone too far. The government is now reversing its official stance on family planning. "While in
70 past decades we controlled the population, over the
next few years we will promote a reasonable growth
rate," says Chien Tai-lang, director of the Department
of Population, Ministry of the Interior.

• Questions for "More Senior Citizens, Fewer Kids"

1. Which two important population factors in Taiwan does this
   article discuss?

   _____

   _____

2. How are these factors expected to affect Taiwan in the future?

   _____

   _____

3. What potential problems might this population shift create?

   _____

   _____

   _____

4. Why is the birthrate declining?

   _____

   _____

   _____

• F. Follow-up Activities

1. Refer to the **Self-Evaluation of Reading Strategies** on pages 120–121. Think about the strategies you used to help yourself understand "Who Lives Longer?" Check off the strategies you used. Think about the strategies you didn't use, and try to apply them to help yourself understand the readings that follow.

2. Look at the following chart carefully; then answer the related questions.

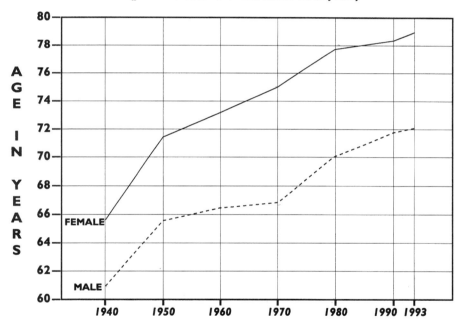

Life Expectancy in the U.S.A.
(years indicated are individuals' birth years)

a. What does this chart illustrate?

_____

b. 1. About how long can a female born in 1970 expect to live? *75*

_____

   2. About how long can a male born in 1970 expect to live? *67*

_____

c. 1. In what decade did life expectancy for males make the greatest gain? How many years did males gain? *70-80*

2. In what decade did life expectancy for females make the greatest gain? How many years did females gain?   *40-50*
   5years

3. In general terms, speculate on what could account for this great increase in life expectancy for *both* sexes in this particular decade.

d. 1. Between 1940 and 1993, what was the overall gain in life expectancy for males?

   2. Between 1940 and 1993, what was the overall gain in life expectancy for females?

3. Look at the following chart carefully; then answer the related questions.

WORLD LIFESPAN HIGHS AND LOWS
(by continent)

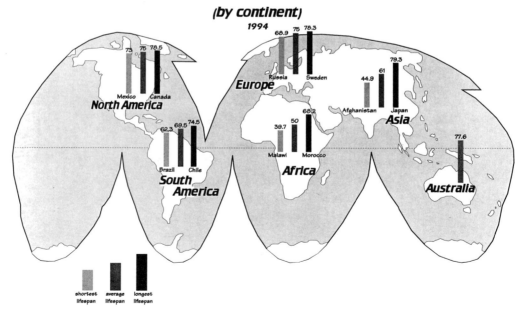

a. What does this chart illustrate?

b. What are some factors that might account for such a world-wide range in life expectancy, e.g., from 39.7 in Malawi or 44.9 in Afghanistan to 79.3 in Japan or 78.3 in Sweden?

_____

_____

4. Work with a partner. Plan a healthy diet for yourselves. Compare your diet with your classmates' diets. As a class, decide which diet is the healthiest.

5. Work with a partner to design a survey to try to predict life expectancy, using the factors that have a positive or negative effect. Include questions about personal behavior (for example, "Do you smoke?"). Ask your classmates and/or other interviewees to respond to your survey. Afterwards you will try to predict how long these people will live. Also, for each person, suggest two changes you believe would result in greater longevity for that person.

• G. Topics for Discussion and Writing

1. What are some of the consequences of an aging population? In other words, what factors must be taken into consideration as the elderly begin to make up a larger segment of a country's population than ever before? What needs will have to be met?

2. In your group, discuss the factors that might shorten a person's life expectancy.

3. Work with two or three other students. In your group, make a list of the steps you can take to increase your life expectancy.

4. Refer to the "World Lifespan Highs and Lows" chart on page 84. Choose a country from the chart. Write a composition about the life expectancy in this country. Include what you think may be reasons for this country's high or low life expectancy.

5. **Write in your journal.** How long would you like to live? Explain your reasons.

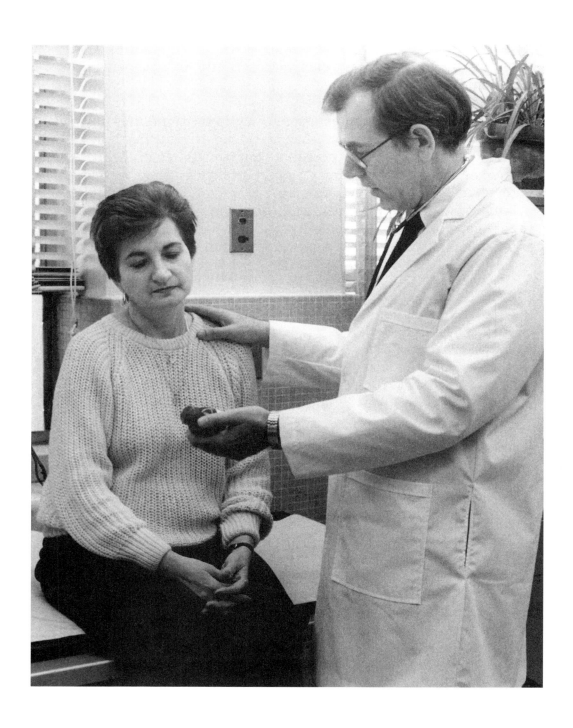

The Mindset of Health

• Prereading Preparation

1. In a small group, look at the photographs of the doctor with two of his patients, on pages 86 and 92. Consider the doctor's demeanor, or behavior, with each patient, and each patient's apparent attitude. What differences do you perceive? How do you think these differences affect the doctor/patient relationship in each case? What do you think about the attitude of each patient towards her treatment?

2. What factors influence good health or bad health? In your group, make a list of factors. When you are finished, compare your list with your classmates' lists. What can you add to your list?

Factors Contributing to Good Health	Factors Contributing to Bad Health

3. A **mindset** is an emotional attitude that influences how a person responds to a situation. What do you think **the mindset of health** means? How might it affect our health?

4. Imagine that you are not feeling well, so you visit your doctor. In your group, describe your office visit in terms of your conversation with your doctor. For example, do you go alone or with someone else? Do you ask the doctor questions if you don't understand? Do you ask about alternative treatments to the one the doctor prescribes? When each of you has described your hypothetical doctor's visit, decide whether your attitude towards your doctor resembles the one you described for the woman on page 86, on page 92, or someone different. When you have finished, decide as a group on the most effective way to talk with your doctor. Discuss your decision with the class. What did you all agree on?

5. Imagine that you want to lose weight. Consider the following contexts and decide which ones are better contexts for staying on a diet. Explain your choices.

   a. a party
   b. lunch at a health food restaurant
   c. lunch at a salad bar
   d. lunch at the home of a friend who is also trying to lose weight
   e. a school cafeteria
   f. a family picnic
   g. dinner in a fast food restaurant
   h. dinner in a good restaurant
   i. dinner at your parents' home
   j. dinner at home alone

6. Read the title of this passage. What do you think this article will be about?

The Mindset of Health

by Ellen J. Langer
Mindfulness

1   Consider this scenario: During a routine physical, your doctor notices a small lump and orders a biopsy as a cancer-screening measure. Your immediate reaction is fear, probably intense fear. Yet in some cases, a tiny
5   lump or mole requires only a tiny incision, comparable to removing a large splinter. Fear in such a situation is based not on the procedure but on your interpretation of what the doctor is doing. You're not thinking about splinters or minor cuts; you're thinking biopsy, cancer, death.
10   From earliest childhood we learn to see mind and body as separate—and to regard the body as without question the more essential of the two. And later, we take our physical problems to one sort of doctor, our mental problems to another. But the mind/body split
15   is not only one of our strongest beliefs, it is a dangerous and premature psychological commitment.
     When we think of various influences on our health, we tend to think of many of them as coming from the outside environment. But each outside influence is me-
20   diated by context. Our perceptions and interpretations influence the ways in which our bodies respond to information in the world. If we automatically —"mindlessly"—accept preconceived notions of the context of a particular situation, we can jeopardize the body's
25   ability to handle that situation. Sometimes, for the sake of our health, we need to place our perceptions intentionally, that is, mindfully in a different context.
     Context can be so powerful that it influences our basic needs. In an experiment on hunger, subjects who
30   chose to fast for a prolonged time for personal reasons tended to be less hungry than those who fasted for external reasons—for money, for example. Freely choosing to perform a task means that one has adopted a certain attitude toward it. In this experiment, those
35   who had made a personal psychological commitment not only were less hungry, but they also showed a smaller increase in free fatty acid levels, a physiological indicator of hunger. The obvious conclusion: State of mind shapes state of body.

Reprinted with permission of Ellen J. Langer. From *Mindfulness*, published by Addison-Wesley.

40   A wide body of recent research has been devoted to investigating the influence of attitudes on the immune system, which is thought to be the intermediary between psychological states and physical illness. The emotional context, our interpretation of the events

45   around us, could thus be the first link in a chain leading to serious illness. And since context is something we can control, the clarification of these links between psychology and illness is good news. Diseases that were once thought to be purely physiological and

50   probably incurable may be more amenable to personal control than we once believed.

Even when a disease may appear to progress inexorably, our reactions to it can be mindful or mindless and thus influence its effects. A very common mindset, as

55   mentioned before, is the conviction that cancer means death. Even if a tumor has not yet had any effect on any body function, or how you feel physically, rarely will you think of yourself as healthy after having a malignancy diagnosed. At the same time, there are almost certainly

60   people walking around with undiagnosed cancer who consider themselves healthy, and may remain so. Yet many doctors have noticed that, following a diagnosis of cancer, some patients seem to go into a decline that has little to do with the actual course of the disease. But they

65   needn't. By reinterpreting the context, they might avoid the unnecessary failure attributable to fear alone.

In recent years there has been much new research that now supports the value of a mindful approach in handling a variety of health situations such as pain. Pa-

70   tients have been successfully taught to tolerate rather severe pain by seeing how pain varies depending on context (thinking of bruises incurred during a football game that are easily tolerated, versus the attention we require to nurse a mere paper cut).

75   This mindful exercise helped the patients get by with fewer pain relievers and sedatives and to leave the hospital earlier than a comparison group of patients. And the results seem to indicate more than a simple, temporary distraction of the mind, because once the

80   stimulus—the source of pain—has been reinterpreted so that the person has a choice of context, one painful, one not, the mind is unlikely to return to the original interpretation. It has, in effect, changed contexts.

We all know people who have quit smoking "cold tur-
85 key." Do they succeed because their commitment to
stop put withdrawal symptoms into a new context?
Jonathan Magolis, a graduate student at Harvard, and I
explored this question in two stages. First we tried to
find out if smokers in a nonsmoking context experi-
90 enced strong cravings for cigarettes. We questioned
smokers in three situations that prohibited smoking: in
a movie theater, at work, and on a religious holiday. The
results in each setting were very similar. People did not
suffer withdrawal symptoms when they were in any of
95 the nonsmoking contexts. But when they returned to a
context where smoking was allowed—a smoke break at
work, for instance—their cravings resurfaced.

All of these people escaped the urge to smoke in a
mindless manner. Could they have achieved the same
100 thing deliberately? Can people control the experience
of temptation?

People who want to stop smoking usually remind
themselves of the health risks, the bad smell, the cost,
others' reactions to their smoking—the drawbacks of
105 smoking. But these effects are not the reasons they
smoke, so trying to quit for those reasons alone often
leads to failure. The problem is that all of the positive
aspects of smoking are still there and still have strong
appeal—the relaxation, the concentration, the taste,
110 the sociable quality of smoking.

A more mindful approach would be to look carefully at these pleasures and find other, less harmful
ways of obtaining them. If the needs served by an addiction or habit can be satisfied in different ways, it
115 would be easier to shake. The deliberate nature of
mindfulness is what makes its potential so enormous.

Whenever we try to heal ourselves and do not abdicate
this responsibility completely to doctors, each step is
mindful. We welcome new information, whether from our
120 bodies or from books. We look at our illness from more
than the single perspective of medicine. We work on
changing contexts, whether it is a stressful workplace or a
depressing view of the hospital. And finally, when we at-
tempt to stay healthy rather than to be made well, we be-
125 come involved in the process rather than the outcome.

There are two ways in which we have learned to influence our health: exchanging unhealthy mindsets for

healthy ones and increasing a generally mindful state. The latter method is more lasting and results in more
130 personal control. Understanding the importance of abandoning the mind/body dualism that has shaped both our thinking and the practice of medicine for so long can make a profound difference in both what we do and how we feel.

135   Consider how you learned to ride a bike. Someone older held on to the seat as you pedaled to keep you from falling until you found your balance. Then, without your knowledge, that strong hand let go and you were riding on your own. You controlled the bicycle
140 without even knowing you had learned how.

    The same is true for all of us most of our lives. We control our health, and the course of disease, without really knowing that we do. But just as on the bike, at some point we all discover that we are in control. Now
145 may be the time for many of us to learn how to recognize and use the control we possess over illness through mindfulness.

• A. Reading Overview: Main Idea, Details, and Summary

Read the passage again. As you read, underline what you think are the most important ideas in the reading. Then, in one or two sentences, write the main idea of the reading. *Use your own words.*

Main idea:

_____

_____

_____

Details:

Use the flowchart below to organize the information in the article. Refer back to the information you underlined in the passage as a guide. When you have finished, write a brief summary of the reading. *Use your own words.*

The Mindset of Health

The Significance of Mindful Attitudes

Context

State of Mind

The Significance of Mindless Attitudes

Context

State of Mind

The importance of context and mindfulness in handling illness

1.

2.

3.

   a.

   b.

Research supporting the effects of mindfulness

1.

2.

How to take a more mindful approach to illness

1.
2.
3.
4.

How to positively influence our health

1.

2.

Summary:

_____

_____

_____

_____

• B. Statement Evaluation

Read the following statements. Then scan the article again quickly to find out if each sentence is **True (T), False (F),** or an **Inference (I).**

1. _____ The people who chose to fast for money were hungrier than those who chose to fast for personal reasons.

2. _____ Researchers have found a clear connection between attitude and illness.

3. _____ New research indicates that a mindful approach may help people handle pain.

4. _____ When smokers were in nonsmoking contexts, they had the urge to smoke.

5. _____ Our mindset influences our health.

6. _____ The way you think sends messages that influence how your body responds.

7. _____ People who quit smoking did not have cigarette cravings in nonsmoking contexts because of their mindset.

• C. Reading Analysis

Read each question carefully. Either circle the letter or number of the correct answer, or write your answer in the space provided.

1. Read lines 20–25.

   a. What word is a synonym of **automatically?**

   _____

   b. These two words mean

      1. carelessly
      2. purposely
      3. without thinking

2. Read lines 25–27.

   a. What word is a synonym of **intentionally?**

   _____

   b. These two synonyms mean

      1. carelessly
      2. purposely
      3. without thinking

   c. What follows **that is** in this sentence?

      1. an explanation of the previous idea
      2. a contrasting idea
      3. a new idea

3. Read lines 29–39.

   a. What does **to fast** mean?

      1. to not eat
      2. to eat
      3. to go quickly

   b. Read **"In an experiment on hunger . . . for example."** In this sentence, what is **money** an example of?

   _____

   c. In this experiment, how did researchers know which subjects were less hungry?

   _____

4. Read lines 67–74. What does **versus** mean?

   a. in addition to
   b. in contrast with
   c. the same as

5. Read lines 75–83.

   a. What is the **stimulus?**

   _____

   b. How do you know?

   _____

6. Read lines 88–95. What follows the colon (:)?

   a. examples
   b. opinions
   c. places

7. Read lines 102–110.

   a. What are the **drawbacks of smoking?**

   _____

   b. What are the **positive aspects of smoking?**

   _____

   c. What is a **drawback?**

      1. an expense
      2. a risk
      3. a disadvantage

8. Read lines 126–130. The **latter method** refers to

   a. exchanging unhealthy mindsets for healthy ones
   b. increasing a generally mindful state

• D. Dictionary Skills

Read the entry for each word, and consider the context of the sentence from the passage. Write the number of the definition that is appropriate for the context on the line next to the word. Be prepared to explain your choice.

1. A large **body** of recent research has been devoted to investigating attitude and the immune system.

   body:_____

   body \'bä-dē\ *n, pl* **bod·ies** [ME, fr. OE *bodig;* akin to OHG *boteh* corpse] (bef. 12c) **1 a** : the main part of a plant or animal body esp. as distinguished from limbs and head : TRUNK **b** : the main, central, or principal part: as (1) : the nave of a church (2) : the bed or box of a vehicle on or in which the load is placed (3) : the enclosed or partly enclosed part of an automobile **2 a** : the organized physical substance of an animal or plant either living or dead: as (1) : the material part or nature of a human being (2) : the dead organism : CORPSE **b** : a human being : PERSON **3 a** : a mass of matter distinct from other masses ⟨a ∼ of water⟩ ⟨a celestial ∼⟩ **b** : something that embodies or gives concrete reality to a thing; *also* : a sensible object in physical space **c** : AGGREGATE, QUANTITY ⟨a ∼ of evidence⟩ **4 a** : the part of a garment covering the body or trunk **b** : the main part of a literary or journalistic work : TEXT 2b **c** : the sound box or pipe of a musical instrument **5** : a group of persons or things: as **a** : a fighting unit : FORCE **b** : a group of individuals organized for some purpose ⟨a legislative ∼⟩ **6 a** : fullness and richness of flavor (as of wine) **b** : VISCOSITY, CONSISTENCY — used esp. of oils and grease **c** : compactness or firmness of texture **d** : fullness or resonance of a musical tone

2. In an experiment on hunger, subjects who chose to fast for a prolonged time for personal reasons tended to be less hungry than those who fasted for external reasons—for money, for example. Freely choosing to perform a task means that one has adopted a certain attitude toward it. In this experiment, those who had made a personal psychological **commitment** were less hungry than the others.

   commitment: _____

   com·mit·ment \kə-'mit-mənt\ *n* (1621) **1 a** : an act of committing to a charge or trust: as (1) : a consignment to a penal or mental institution (2) : an act of referring a matter to a legislative committee **b** : MITTIMUS **2 a** : an agreement or pledge to do something in the future; *esp* : an engagement to assume a financial obligation at a future date **b** : something pledged **c** : the state or an instance of being obligated or emotionally impelled ⟨a ∼ to a cause⟩

Pronunciation Guide

\ə\ **abut** \ˀ\ **kitten,** F **table** \ər\ **further** \a\ **ash** \ā\ **ace** \ä\ **mop, mar**
\aú\ **out** \ch\ **chin** \e\ **bet** \ē\ **easy** \g\ **go** \i\ **hit** \ī\ **ice** \j\ **job**
\ŋ\ **sing** \ō\ **go** \ò\ **law** \òi\ **boy** \th\ **thin** \th̲\ **the** \ü\ **loot** \ú\ **foot**
\y\ **yet** \zh\ **vision** \à, k̲, ⁿ, œ. œ̃. ɪ̄e. ī̄e. ʸ\

3. We control our health, and the **course** of illness, without really knowing that we do. In fact, many doctors have noticed that, following a diagnosis of cancer, some patients seem to go into a decline that has little to do with the actual **course** of the disease.

course: _____

course \\'kōrs, 'kȯrs\ *n* [ME, fr OF, fr. L *cursus,* fr. *currere* to run — more at CAR] (14c) **1** : the act or action of moving in a path from point to point **2** : the path over which something moves or extends: as **a** : RACECOURSE **b** (1) : the direction of travel of a vehicle (as a ship or airplane) usu. measured as a clockwise angle from north; *also* : the projected path of travel (2) : a point of the compass **c** : WATER-COURSE **d** : GOLF COURSE **3** **a** : accustomed procedure or normal action ⟨the law taking its ∼⟩ **b** : a chosen manner of conducting oneself : way of acting ⟨our wisest ∼ is to retreat⟩ **c** (1) : progression through a development or period or a series of acts or events (2) : LIFE HISTORY, CAREER **4** : an ordered process or succession: as **a** : a number of lectures or other matter dealing with a subject; *also* : a series of such courses constituting a curriculum ⟨a premed ∼⟩ **b** : a series of doses or medications administered over a designated period **5** **a** : a part of a meal served at one time **b** : LAYER; *esp* : a continuous level range of brick or masonry throughout a wall **c** : the lowest sail on a square-rigged mast — **in due course** : after a normal passage of time : in the expected or allotted time — **of course** **1** : following the ordinary way or procedure **2** : as might be expected

4. Our perceptions influence how our bodies respond to information in the world. If we automatically—mindlessly"—accept preconceived **notions** of the context of a particular situation, we can jeopardize the body's ability to handle that situation.

notion: _____

no·tion \\'nō-shən\ *n* [L *notion-, notio,* fr. *noscere*] (1537) **1 a** (1) : an individual's conception or impression of something known, experienced, or imagined (2) : an inclusive general concept (3) : a theory or belief held by a person or group **b** : a personal inclination : WHIM **2** *obs* : MIND, INTELLECT **3** *pl* : small useful items : SUNDRIES *syn* see IDEA

• E. Critical Thinking

Read each question carefully. Write your response in the space provided. Remember that there is no one correct answer. Your response depends on what **you** think.

1. Read this sentence: "The emotional context, our interpretation of the events around us, could thus be the first link in a chain leading to serious illness." The author is comparing links in a chain in order to describe the chain of events from our emotional context to a serious illness. What do you think this chain of events is? How can this chain of events be broken at any given step on the way to serious illness?

   _____

   _____

   _____

   _____

2. Read this sentence: "Diseases that were once thought to be purely physiological and probably incurable may be more amenable to personal control than we once believed." What kind of effect might personal control have on these diseases? What diseases do you think we might be able to control in this way?

   _____

   _____

   _____

   _____

3. Read the paragraph regarding teaching patients to deal with pain. The author states that these patients were able to "get by with fewer pain relievers and sedatives and to leave the hospital earlier than a comparison group of patients." Who was the other, comparison, group of patients? Why were two groups of patients used in this research? Is this a valid method of research? Why or why not?

   _____

   _____

   _____

   _____

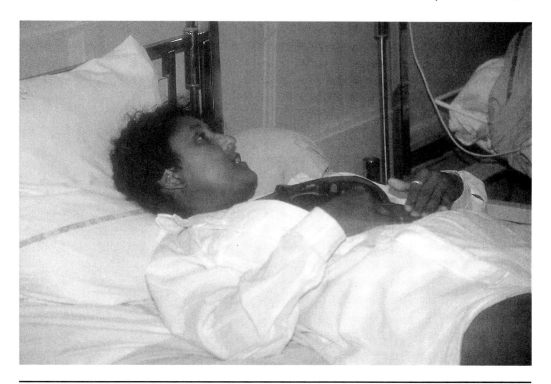

• Another Perspective

How to Behave in a Hospital

by Gloria Emerson
American Health

1   Appear to be submissive, humble, grateful and un-demanding. Show unbridled pleasure if a doctor comes into your room, even if the visit is brief and useless. Be courteous to all nurses and others on the staff. Give
5 thanks often. Do not challenge anyone with authority unless you are famous, very rich, a member of at least a minor royal family or related to a head of state.

    Stay alert. For example, when medicine is handed out, the names of patients are usually written on the
10 bottoms of the paper cups holding the pills. If your name is Walters, do not accept medicine designated for Alvarez. Tactfully point out the mistake, pretending that your eyesight is poor and you may be muddled.

    These are a few strategies—offered after 12 days in
15 a hospital in Princeton, N.J., and another 12 days in a huge teaching hospital in New York City—for dealing with today's American medical establishment.

What patients want is to be treated with respect and consideration, which in my experience too few hospi-
20 tals and doctors bestow. In his book *A Whole New Life*, novelist Reynolds Price recalls that his doctors chose a crowded hallway as the place to tell him he might have a tumor on his spinal cord. It did not occur to the two physicians that a "hallway mob scene" was not the most
25 appropriate venue for that particular piece of news. Price writes of the "well-known but endlessly deplorable and faceless—near criminal—nature of so much current medicine."

In the operating room of the Princeton hospital
30 where my profoundly fractured hip is to be repaired, I listen to the anesthesiologist chattering to a colleague about the pastrami sandwiches served by a local delicatessen. A few days later, the same anesthesiologist telephones to say that he has seen, in a bookstore, one
35 of the books I have written and wants to know how I feel. I thank him. But he has not fooled me; I know that he mistakenly thinks I'm an important person and wishes only to ingratiate himself.

My surgeon, who is in his mid 30s, looks tired: He
40 has been overwhelmed with patients who have fallen on the treacherous winter ice, his beeper is going off every 15 minutes. He is a witty man, but sometimes his wit is unwelcome.

"Blue Cross[1] wants me to put you out in the snow
45 tomorrow afternoon," he tells me after I have been in the hospital for more than a week. I'm terrified, because I have no idea where to go. I cannot walk, or even lift my leg a few inches. The hospital social worker strikes me as an idiot, but my complaints about
50 her only annoy my surgeon. "I have to work with these people," he tells my friend Dr. Karen Brudney when she mercifully intercedes on my behalf and arranges for me to be transferred to another hospital.

"If you say one negative thing, they get defensive,"
55 she tells me later. "They have this kind of institutional loyalty." Brudney told me: "Always bring an advocate— that is, any other person—with you to the hospital, and write everything down, every single question and the answer, the name of every doctor and nurse. When

---

[1]   Blue Cross is a major health insurance company.

60 people know you have their names, they behave better."

Since it is not wise to be regarded as a whiner or to be too demanding (the nurses begin to ignore you or take longer in coming to your room) Brudney—my advocate—advises cunning strategies. "You can frame your
65 questions as those of a frightened patient. For example, 'Do you think my foot should really hurt this much?'"

And Brudney adds: "If you, as a patient, suggest that you might like to control even part of the situation or be consulted or informed, then you are consid-
70 ered difficult. They want you to be totally passive. The entire health care system, particularly hospitals and nursing homes, exists for reasons that have nothing to do with taking care of patients. Patients are incidental."

• Questions for "How to Behave in a Hospital"

1. How does Gloria Emerson suggest we behave in a hospital?

   _____

   _____

   _____

2. In a hospital, if someone gives us the wrong medicine, according to Ms. Emerson, how should we react?

   _____

   _____

   _____

3. How do Gloria Emerson and Ellen Langer differ in their ideas about how we should behave in hospitals, or with doctors in general?

   _____

   _____

   _____

• F. Follow-up Activities

1. Refer to the **Self-Evaluation of Reading Strategies** on pages 120–121. Think about the strategies you used to help yourself understand "The Mindset of Health." Check off the strategies you used. Think about the strategies you didn't use, and try to apply them to help yourself understand the readings that follow.

2. The tendency in the United States to go to different people for our emotional and physical problems is not universal. Some cultures treat the person holistically. In a small group, compare health care in your country with that in the United States and in the countries of your classmates. How are they similar? How are they different?

3. Work with a partner. One person will act the role of a doctor, and the other person will act the role of a patient. The patient will want to lose weight or stop smoking, or some other reason you choose. Work together to set up a mindful context to help the person achieve this goal. Include specific information about the reason why this person wants to lose weight or stop smoking, as well as which situations the patient should avoid and which situations would be helpful for the patient to be in to help him or her achieve the goal.

4. Work in pairs. Discuss how Gloria Emerson's suggestions for behavior differ from Ellen Langer's. Which approach is mindful? Which approach is mindless? Compare your responses with your classmates'. Do you all have the same responses?

• G. Topics for Discussion and Writing

1. Researchers are investigating the influence of attitude on the immune system. What effect do you think the mind has on the body? Do you think there is a connection? How are they connected?

2. Gloria Emerson described an atmosphere that is common in many hospitals today. How can we ensure that we are treated well in a hospital and that we get the information about our medication and treatment that we need?

3. **Write in your journal.** Describe a time in your life when you needed medical help. How did you respond emotionally to your illness and to the doctor? Did you have a mindful or a mindless attitude? Do you think you would respond differently now after reading these two articles? Explain your answer.

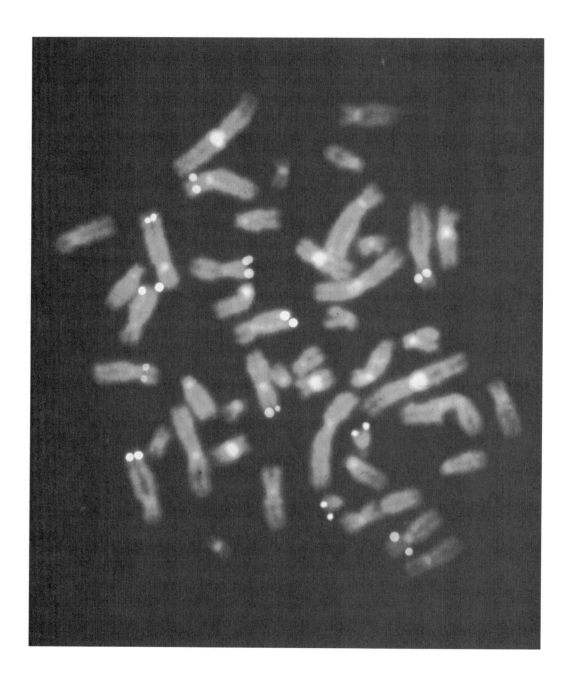

My Genes Made Me Do It

• Prereading Preparation

Read the following summary of the article "My Genes Made Me Do It."

Americans are increasingly likely to attribute their own—and others'—behavior to innate biological causes. At best that may relieve guilt about behavior we want to change but can't. The quest for genetic explanations of why we do what we do more accurately reflects the desire for hard certainties about frightening societal problems than the true complexities of human affairs. Meanwhile, the revolution in thinking about genes has huge consequences for how we view ourselves.

1. Complete the following chart. Which human traits or characteristics do you think are genetic (inherited)? Which do you think are environmental, and therefore controllable? When you are done, compare your answers with your classmates'.

Genetic Traits	Non-Genetic Traits
1.	1.
2.	2.
3.	3.
4.	4.
5.	5.
6.	6.

2. Read the title of this article. What aspect of human behavior do you think the article will examine?

My Genes Made Me Do It

by Stanton Peele and Richard DeGrandpre
Psychology Today

1   Just about every week now, we read a newspaper headline about the genetic basis for cancer, intelligence, or obesity. In previous years, these stories were about the genes for alcoholism, schizophrenia, and
5   manic-depression. Such news stories may lead us to believe our lives are being revolutionized by genetic discoveries. We may be on the verge of reversing and eliminating mental illness, for example. In addition, many believe, we can identify the causes of criminality,
10   personality, and other basic human foibles and traits.

But these hopes, it turns out, are based on faulty assumptions about genes and behavior. Although genetic research wears the mantle of science, most of the headlines are more hype[1] than reality. Many discover-
15   ies loudly touted to the public have been quietly refuted by further research. Other scientifically valid discoveries—like the gene for breast cancer—have nonetheless fallen short of initial claims.

The public is hard pressed to evaluate which traits
20   are genetically inspired based on the validity of scientific research. In many cases, people are motivated to accept research claims by the hope of finding solutions for frightening problems, like breast cancer, that our society has failed to solve. At a personal level, people wonder
25   about how much actual choice they have in their lives. Accepting genetic causes for their traits can relieve guilt about behavior they want to change, but can't.

These psychological forces influence how we view mental illnesses like schizophrenia and depression, so-
30   cial problems like criminality, and personal maladies like obesity and bulimia. All have grown unabated in recent decades. Efforts made to combat them, at growing expense, have made little or no visible progress. The public wants to hear that science can help, while scien-
35   tists want to prove that they have remedies for problems that eat away at our individual and social well-being.

Meanwhile, genetic claims are being made for a host of ordinary and abnormal behaviors, from addic-

---

[1] Hype is a term used to describe exaggerated claims or publicity.

Reprinted with permission from Stanton Peele, excerpt from *Psychology Today*, July/August 1995.

tion to shyness and even to political views and di-
40 vorce. If who we are is determined from conception,
then our efforts to change or to influence our children
may be futile. There may also be no basis for insisting
that people behave themselves and conform to laws.
Thus, the revolution in thinking about genes has mon-
45 umental consequences for how we view ourselves as
human beings.

Most claims linking emotional disorders and behaviors to genes are statistical in nature. For example, differences in the correlations in traits between identical
50 twins (who inherit identical genes) and fraternal twins
(who have half their genes in common) are examined
with the goal of separating the role of environment
from that of genes. But this goal is elusive. Research
finds that identical twins are treated more alike than
55 fraternal twins. These calculations are therefore insuf-
ficient for deciding that alcoholism or manic-depression is inherited, let alone television viewing,
conservatism, and other basic, everyday traits for
which such claims have been made.

60 In the late 1980s, genes for schizophrenia and
manic-depression were identified with great fanfare by
teams of geneticists. Both claims have now been defini-
tively disproved. Yet, while the original announce-
ments were heralded on TV news and front pages of
65 newspapers around the country, most people are un-
aware of the refutations.

In 1987, the prestigious British journal *Nature* published an article linking manic-depression to a specific
gene. This conclusion came from family linkage stud-
70 ies, which search for gene variants in suspect sections
on the chromosomes of families with a high incidence
of a disease. Usually, an active area of DNA (called a
genetic marker) is observed to coincide with the disease. If the same marker appears only in diseased fam-
75 ily members, evidence of a genetic link has been
established. Even so, this does not guarantee that a
gene can be identified with the marker.

One genetic marker of manic-depression was identified in a single extended Amish[2] family. But this
80 marker was not apparent in other families that dis-

---

[2] Amish people are a cultural group in the United States. They
marry strictly within their society, which is not large in number.

played the disorder. Then, further evaluations placed several members of the family without the marker in the manic-depressive category. Another marker de-tected in several Israeli families was subjected to more
85 detailed genetic analysis, and a number of subjects were switched between the marked and unmarked cat-egories. Ultimately, those with and without the puta-tive markers had similar rates of the disorder.

Epidemiologic (genetic) data on the major mental
90 illnesses make it clear that they can't be reduced to purely genetic causes. For example, according to psy-chiatric epidemiologist Myrna Weissman, Ph.D., Ameri-cans born before 1905 had a 1 percent rate of depression by age 75. Among Americans born a half
95 century later, six percent became depressed by age 24! Similarly, while the average age at which manic-depres-sion first appears was 32 in the mid 1960s, its average onset today is 19. Only social factors can produce such large shifts in incidence and age of onset of mental
100 disorders in a few decades.

The inextricable interplay between genes and envi-ronment is evident in disorders like alcoholism, anor-exia, or overeating that are characterized by abnormal behaviors. Scientists spiritedly debate whether such
105 syndromes are more or less biologically driven. If they are mainly biological—rather than psychological, so-cial, and cultural—then there may be a genetic basis for them. Therefore, there was considerable interest in the announcement of the discovery of an "alcoholism
110 gene" in 1990. Kenneth Blum, Ph.D., of the University of Texas, and Ernest Noble, M.D., of the University of California, Los Angeles, found a certain gene in 70 per-cent of a group of alcoholics—these were cadavers—but in only 20 percent of a non-alcoholic group.
115 The Blum-Noble discovery was broadcast around the country after being published in the *Journal of the American Medical Association* (JAMA). But, in a 1993 JAMA article, Joel Gelernter, M.D., of Yale and his col-leagues surveyed all the studies that examined this
120 gene and alcoholism. Discounting Blum and Noble's re-search, the combined results were that 18 percent of non-alcoholics, 18 percent of problem drinkers, and 18 percent of severe alcoholics *all* had the gene. There was simply no link between this gene and alcoholism!

125   The dubious state of Blum and Noble's work does
not disprove that a gene—or set of genes—could trig-
ger alcoholism. A more plausible model is that genes
may affect how people experience alcohol. Perhaps
drinking is more rewarding for alcoholics. Perhaps
130 some people's neurotransmitters are more activated by
alcohol. But although genes can influence reactions to
alcohol, they cannot explain why some people continue drinking to the point of destroying their lives.

How much freedom each person has to develop re-
135 turns us to the issue of whether nature and nurture can
be separated. The goal of determining what portion of
behavior is genetic and environmental will always
elude us. Our personalities and destinies don't evolve
in this straightforward manner. Claims that our genes
140 cause our problems, our misbehavior, even our personalities are more a mirror of our culture's attitudes than
a window for human understanding and change.

• A. Reading Overview: Main Idea, Details, and Summary

Read the passage again. As you read, underline what you think are
the most important ideas in the reading. Then, in one or two sentences, write the main idea of the reading. *Use your own words.*

Main idea:

_____

_____

_____

Details:

Use the chart below to organize the information in the article. Refer back to the information you underlined in the passage as a guide. When you have finished, write a brief summary of the reading. *Use your own words.*

My Genes Made Me Do It

Personality Trait or Behavior Discussed in This Article	Scientists' Conclusions About This Trait or Behavior

Summary:

_____

_____

_____

_____

_____

• B. Statement Evaluation

Read the following statements. Then scan the article again quickly to find out if each sentence is **True (T), False (F),** or **Not Mentioned (NM)** in the article..

1. _____ If all our characteristics and traits are genetic, then we can change our children's behavior.

2. _____ Researchers want to separate genetic and environmental causes of behavior, so they study the differences in traits in twins.

3. _____ Researchers look for proof of a genetic link if a genetic marker appears only in diseased family members.

4. _____ Scientists have found a gene that causes overeating.

5. _____ An "alcoholism gene" explains why some people destroy their lives by drinking.

6. _____ In the near future, researchers will find a genetic link for all our problems and personality traits.

• C. Reading Analysis

Read each question carefully. Either circle the letter or number of the correct answer, or write your answer in the space provided.

1. Read lines 1–18.

   a. **On the verge of** means

      1. capable of
      2. at the point of
      3. incapable of

   b. **These hopes** refers to

      _____

   c. **Faulty assumptions** are

      1. facts
      2. untrue beliefs
      3. incorrect genes

   d. **Loudly touted** and **quietly refuted** are

      1. contrasting actions
      2. similar ideas

2. Read lines 24–27. **"Accepting genetic causes for their traits can relieve guilt about behavior they want to change, but can't"** means

   a. people can blame their unwanted behavior on their genes
   b. people can change their unwanted behavior
   c. genes for unwanted behavior make some people feel guilty

3. Read lines 28–36.

   a. What does **All** refer to (line 31)?

      _____

   b. **Grown unabated** means

      1. finally stopped
      2. increased without control
      3. slowly decreasing

   c. Efforts made to combat them have been

      1. successful
      2. unsuccessful

4. Read lines 60–66. What happened after the genes for schizophrenia and manic-depression were identified?

   a. The claims were proven to be wrong.
   b. Many people were cured.
   c. The claims were supported by more research.

5. Read lines 67–77. What were the results of the research on the genetic marker of manic-depression?

   a. The research showed that the marker appeared only in people who were manic-depressive.
   b. The research showed that the marker sometimes didn't appear in people who were manic-depressive.

6. Read lines 89–100. According to this paragraph, what is the cause of the increase in depression?

   a. genetic factors
   b. societal factors

7. Read lines 115–124. Why did Dr. Gelernter and his colleagues believe that **"there was simply no link between this gene and alcoholism!"**

   a. Because 18 percent of severe alcoholics had the gene.
   b. Because 18 percent of problem drinkers had the gene.
   c. Because 18 percent of alcoholics and 18 percent of non-alcoholics had the gene.

8. Read lines 136–142. In these sentences, what words are synonyms for **nature and nurture?**

• D. Dictionary Skills

Read the entry for each word, and consider the context of the sentence from the passage. Write the number of the definition that is appropriate for the context on the line next to the word. Write the entry number too when appropriate. Be prepared to explain your choice.

1. Certain psychological forces influence how we view mental illnesses, social problems, and personal maladies. All have grown unabated in recent decades. Efforts made to **combat** them have made little or no visible progress.

   combat: _____

   > ¹**com·bat** \'käm-,bat\ *n* (1546)   **1 :** a fight or contest between individuals or groups   **2 :** CONFLICT, CONTROVERSY   **3 :** active fighting in a war : ACTION ⟨casualties suffered in ∼⟩
   > ²**com·bat** \kəm-'bat, 'käm-,\ *vb* **-bat·ed** *or* **-bat·ted; -bat·ing** *or* **-bat·ting** [MF *combattre,* fr. (assumed) VL *combattere,* fr. L *com-* + *battuere* to beat] *vi* (1564) **:** to engage in combat : FIGHT   ∼ *vt* **1 :** to fight with : BATTLE   **2 :** to struggle against; *esp* **:** to strive to reduce or eliminate ⟨∼ pollution⟩   ***syn*** see OPPOSE
   > ³**com·bat** \'käm-,bat\ *adj* (1825)   **1 :** relating to combat ⟨∼ missions⟩   **2 :** designed or destined for combat ⟨∼ boots⟩ ⟨∼ troops⟩

2. In a 1993 JAMA article, Joel Gelernter and his colleagues surveyed all the studies that examined the "alcoholism gene" and alcoholism. They **discounted** Blum and Noble's research because the combined results indicated that there was simply no link between this gene and alcoholism.

   discount: _____

   > **dis·count** \'dis-,kaůnt, dis-'\ *vb* [modif. of F *décompter,* fr. OF *desconter,* fr. ML *discomputare,* fr. L *dis-* + *computare* to count — more at COUNT] *vt* (1629)   **1   a :** to make a deduction from usu. for cash or prompt payment   **b :** to sell or offer for sale at a discount   **2 :** to lend money on after deducting the discount   **3   a :** to leave out of account : DISREGARD   **b :** to minimize the importance of   **c** (1) **:** to make allowance for bias or exaggeration in   (2) **:** to view with doubt   **d :** to take into account (as a future event) in present calculations   ∼ *vi* **:** to give or make discounts — **dis·count·er** \-,kaůn-tər, -'kaůn-\ *n*

Pronunciation Guide

\ə\ **abut** \'ⁿ\ **kitten,** F **table** \ər\ **further** \a\ **ash** \ā\ **ace** \ä\ **mop, mar**
\aů\ **out** \ch\ **chin** \e\ **bet** \ē\ **easy** \g\ **go** \i\ **hit** \ī\ **ice** \j\ **job**
\ŋ\ **sing** \ō\ **go** \ȯ\ **law** \ȯi\ **boy** \th\ **thin** \t̲h̲\ **the** \ü\ **loot** \ů\ **foot**
\y\ **yet** \zh\ **vision** \à, k̲, ⁿ, œ, œ̄, ʊ, ʊ̄, ʸ\

3. Genetic claims are being made for a **host** of ordinary and abnormal behaviors, from addiction to shyness and even to political views and divorce.

host: _____

¹host \'hōst\ *n* [ME, fr. OF, fr. LL *hostis,* fr. L, stranger, enemy — more at GUEST] (14c) **1 :** ARMY **2 :** a very large number : MULTITUDE
²host *vi* (15c) **:** to assemble in a host usu. for a hostile purpose
³host *n* [ME *hoste* host, guest, fr. OF, fr. L *hospit-, hospes,* prob. fr. *hostis*] (14c) **1 a :** one that receives or entertains guests socially, commercially, or officially **b :** one that provides facilities for an event or function ⟨our college served as ∼ for the basketball tournament⟩ **2 a :** a living animal or plant affording subsistence or lodgment to a parasite **b :** the larger, stronger, or dominant member of a commensal or symbiotic pair **c :** an individual into which a tissue, part, or embryo is transplanted from another **3 :** a mineral or rock that is older than the minerals or rocks in it; *also* **:** a substance that contains a usu. small amount of another substance incorporated in its structure **4 :** a radio or television emcee **5 :** a computer that controls communications in a network that administers a database

4. Only social factors can produce such large **shifts** in the incidence and age of onset of mental disorders in a few decades.

shift: _____

¹shift \'shift\ *vb* [ME, fr. OE *sciftan* to divide, arrange; akin to ON *skipa* to arrange, assign] *vt* (13c) **1 :** to exchange for or replace by another : CHANGE **2 a :** to change the place, position, or direction of : MOVE **b :** to make a change in (place) **3 :** to change phonetically ∼ *vi* **1 a :** to change place or position **b :** to change direction ⟨the wind ∼*ed*⟩ **c :** to change gears **d :** to depress the shift key (as on a typewriter) **2 a :** to assume responsibility ⟨had to ∼ for themselves⟩ **b :** to resort to expedients **3 a :** to go through a change **b :** to change one's clothes **c :** to become changed phonetically — **shift-able** \'shif-tə-bəl\ *adj* — **shift·er** *n* — **shift gears :** to make a change
²shift *n* (1523) **1 a :** a means or device for effecting an end **b** (1) **:** a deceitful or underhand scheme : DODGE (2) **:** an expedient tried in difficult circumstances : EXTREMITY **2 a** *chiefly dial* **:** a change of clothes **b** (1) *chiefly dial* **:** SHIRT (2) **:** a woman's slip or chemise (3) **:** a usu. loose-fitting or semifitted dress **3 a :** a change in direction ⟨a ∼ in the wind⟩ **b :** a change in emphasis, judgment, or attitude **4 a :** a group of people who work or occupy themselves in turn with other groups **b** (1) **:** a change of one group of people (as workers) for another in regular alternation (2) **:** a scheduled period of work or duty **5 :** a change in place or position: as **a :** a change in the position of the hand on a fingerboard (as of a violin) **b** (1) **:** FAULT 5 (2) **:** the relative displacement of rock masses on opposite sides of a fault or fault zone **c** (1) **:** a simultaneous change of position in football by two or more players from one side of the line to the other (2) **:** a change of positions made by one or more players in baseball to provide better defense against a particular hitter **d :** a change in frequency resulting in a change in position of a spectral line or band — compare DOPPLER EFFECT **e :** a movement of bits in a computer register a specified number of places to the right or left **6 :** a removal from one person or thing to another : TRANSFER **7 :** CONSONANT SHIFT **8 :** a bid in bridge in a suit other than the suit one's partner has bid — compare JUMP **9 :** GEARSHIFT *syn* see RESOURCE

• E. Critical Thinking

Read each question carefully. Write your response in the space provided. Remember that there is no one correct answer. Your response
depends on what **you** think.

1. The authors state that "the public is hard pressed to evaluate
   which traits are genetically inspired based on the validity of
   scientific research." Why would it be difficult for the public to
   evaluate these studies?

   _____

   _____

   _____

2. Why does "the public want to hear that science can help, while
   scientists want to prove that they have remedies for problems
   that eat away at our individual and social well-being"?

   _____

   _____

   _____

3. The two genes for schizophrenia and for manic-depression that
   were identified by team of geneticists have now been defini-
   tively disproved. Why do you think that most people are un-
   aware that this finding has been disproved?

   _____

   _____

   _____

4. Why was the genetic marker for manic-depression unreliable?

   _____

   _____

   _____

5. The authors state that "claims that our genes cause our problems, our misbehavior, even our personalities are more a mirror
   of our culture's attitudes. . . ." What do the authors believe
   about our culture's attitudes?

   _____

   _____

   _____

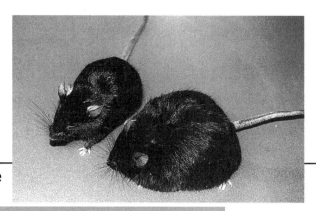

• Another Perspective

Of (Fat) Mice and Men (*excerpt from* My Genes Made Me Do It)

1   Public interest was aroused by the 1995 announcement by Rockefeller University geneticist Jeffrey Friedman, M.D., of a genetic mutation in obese mice. The
researchers believe this gene influences development
5 of a hormone that tells the organism how fat or full it
is. Those with the mutation may not sense when they
have achieved satiety or if they have sufficient fatty
tissue, and thus can't tell when to stop eating.
   The researchers also reported finding a gene nearly
10 identical to the mouse obesity gene in humans. The operation of this gene in humans has not yet been demonstrated, however. Still, professionals like University of
Vermont psychologist Esther Rothblum, Ph.D., reacted
enthusiastically: "This research indicates that people re-
15 ally are born with a tendency to have a certain weight,
just as they are to have a particular skin color or height."
   Actually, behavioral geneticists believe that less than
half of total weight variation is programmed in the
genes, while height is almost entirely genetically deter-
20 mined. Whatever role genes play, America is getting fat-
ter. A survey by the Center for Disease Control found
that obesity has increased greatly over the last 10 years.
Such rapid change underlines the role of environmental
factors, like the abundance of rich foods, in America's
25 overeating. The CDC has also found that teens are far
less physically active than they were even a decade ago.
   Accepting that weight is predetermined can relieve
guilt for overweight people. But people's belief that
they cannot control their weight can itself contribute
30 to obesity.

• Questions for "Of (Fat) Mice and Men"

1. What announcement did Dr. Friedman make?

   _____

   _____

2. How does this mutation affect the mice?

   _____

   _____

3. Do behavioral geneticists agree with these findings? Explain your answer.

   _____

   _____

4. What other factors might account for obesity in humans?

   _____

   _____

5. Why might the belief that weight is predetermined be a disadvantage to people?

   _____

   _____

• F. Follow-up Activities

1. Refer to the **Self-Evaluation of Reading Strategies** on the next page. Think about the strategies you used to help yourself understand "My Genes Made Me Do It." Check off the strategies you used. Evaluate your strategy use over the first six chapters. Which strategies have you begun to use that you didn't use before? Which strategies do you use consistently? Which strategies have you added to the list? Which strategies are becoming automatic? To what extent have you applied these strategies to other reading you do?

Self-Evaluation Of Reading Strategies

	Readings		
Strategies	"Who Lives Longer?"	"The Mindset of Health"	"My Genes Made Me Do It"
I read the title and try to predict what the reading will be about.			
I use my knowledge of the world to help me understand the text.			
I read as though I *expect* the text to have meaning.			
I use illustrations to help me understand the text.			
I ask myself questions about the text.			
I use a variety of types of context clues.			
I take chances in order to identify meaning.			
I continue if I am not successful.			
I identify and underline main ideas.			
I connect details with main ideas.			
I summarize the reading in my own words.			
I skip unnecessary words.			
I look up words correctly in the dictionary.			
I connect the reading to other material I have read.			
I do not translate into my native language.			

2. Look at the following graph carefully, then answer the related questions.

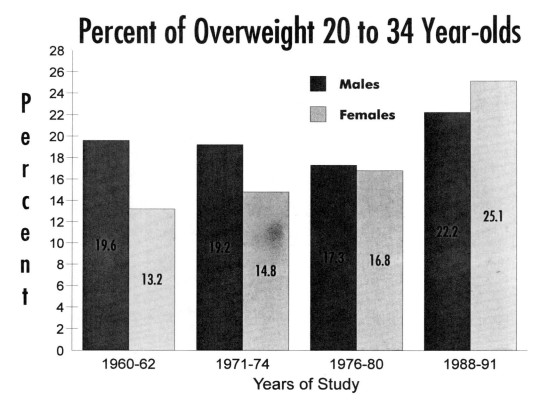

Percent of Overweight 20 to 34 Year-olds

Males
Females

19.6 13.2 19.2 14.8 17.3 16.8 22.2 25.1

1960-62   1971-74   1976-80   1988-91

Years of Study

a. What does this graph illustrate?

_____

b. Describe what this graph indicates with regard to overweight females.

_____

c. Describe what this graph indicates with regard to overweight males.

_____

d. What trend does this graph seem to indicate?

_____

3. As a class, choose three physical or personality traits to discuss. Work in an even number of groups. Half of the groups will discuss the implications of the theory that genetics (i.e., nature) causes the behaviors and traits you have chosen. The other half of the groups will discuss the implications of the theory that environment (i.e., nurture) causes these behaviors and traits. Write on the blackboard your explanations for nature or nurture for each trait. As a class, decide whether genetics or environment has a stronger influence on our behavior.

• G. Topics for Discussion and Writing

1. Refer back to the chart on page 122. Do the statistics in this chart tend to support or contradict researchers' claims that obesity is genetic? Explain your answer, and discuss it with your classmates.

2. In your country, do people tend to attribute their negative traits or behaviors to genetics or to environment? Write a composition explaining your response.

3. **Write in your journal.** Is there something about yourself that you would like to change? Do you think it is possible for you to change this trait? Explain your reasons.

Unit II Review

• H. Crossword Puzzle

• Crossword Puzzle Clues

Across

2. showing good sense
6. in contrast with
8. connection
11. deliberately
13. a promise to do something
14. _____ refers to biology, i.e., heredity
15. struggle against
17. an event marking a turning point
21. to not eat
22. a disadvantage
23. uncontrolled
24. a voice
25. _____ refers to the heart

Down

1. the progression through a development of acts or events
3. an idea, theory, or belief that a person holds
4. a theory
5. characteristic
7. a change
9. a vital or crucial element
10. all-compassing; deep
12. without thought or conscious action
16. guess; belief
18. view with doubt; disbelieve
19. unchangeable
20. _____ refers to our environment, to how we are raised

Technology and Ethical Issues

C · H · A · P · T · E · R 7

Assisted Suicide:
Multiple Perspectives

• Prereading Preparation

1. This chapter presents a variety of perspectives on assisted suicide. Work with a partner or in a small group. Make a list of the different people who might have different viewpoints on assisted suicide. When you are finished, compare your list with your classmates'.

2. Dr. Timothy Quill of the University of Rochester has revealed publicly that he prescribed sleeping pills for Diane, a patient dying of leukemia, knowing that she would use them to end her life. He discussed his decision with *U.S. News's* Amy Bernstein. Below are the questions that she asked him. What do you think were his answers? Work with a partner and discuss what you think he replied. When you are finished, read Dr. Quill's actual answers on the next page and compare them to your own.

Amy Bernstein's Questions

a. How did you make your decision?

_____

_____

b. Have you had second thoughts?

_____

_____

c. Do doctors often assist in suicides?

_____

_____

d. What are the legal consequences? *result.*

_____

_____

Reprinted with permission of *U.S. News & World Report*, *Q & A: Mercy Mission*, Amy Bernstein, March 18, 1991.

Dr. Quill's answers:

a. I knew Diane very well and was sure all avenues had been explored. Her alternatives were to tolerate increasing pain and fevers or to be heavily sedated—states worse than death. Sometimes, all one can look forward to is suffering, and our job is to try to lessen that in any way the patient wants. We may not be able to do some things because of personal beliefs, but the goal is to make the patient comfortable—and she defines what that entails, not the doctor.

b. I think about it a lot. I talked to a whole lot of people about it. But I think she got the best care possible.

c. Many doctors have a similar story—a secret about a very personal commitment to a patient that went to the edges of what's accepted.

d. It's a personal, not a legal, matter. This should be debated among clinicians and bioethicists. One purpose of what I did is to have that debate occur with a real case, with a real person who makes a very strong argument. Diane's gone. But there are many Dianes out there.

3. Compare your answers with the answers Dr. Quill gave Ms. Bernstein. Which answers were similar? Which were different?

4. As a member of the medical profession, Dr. Quill offers a particular perspective on assisted suicide. What other perspectives might a doctor have on this issue?

5. Read the following excerpt from a book written by Dr. Francis Moore. When you finish reading, consider the viewpoints of both Dr. Quill and Dr. Moore. What do each of these doctors consider with regard to the issue of assisted suicide?

Matters of Life and Death

1   *In a new book,* A Miracle and a Privilege *(Joseph Henry Press/National Academy Press), Dr. Francis Moore, 81, of Harvard Medical School, discusses a lifetime of grappling with the issue of when to help a patient die. An excerpt:*

5   Doctors of our generation are not newcomers to this question. Going back to my internship days, I can remember many patients in pain, sometimes in coma or delirious, with late, hopeless cancer. For many of them, we wrote an order for heavy medication—morphine[1] by

10 the clock. This was not talked about openly and little was written about it. It was essential, not controversial.

    The best way to bring the problem into focus is to describe two patients whom I cared for. The first, formerly a nurse, had sustained a fractured pelvis in an automo-

15 bile accident. A few days later her lungs seemed to fill up; her urine stopped; her heart developed dangerous rhythm disturbances. So there she was: in coma, on dialysis, on a breathing machine, her heartbeat maintained with an electrical device. One day after rounds, my sec-

20 retary said the husband and son of the patient wanted to see me. They told me their wife and mother was obviously going to die; she was a nurse and had told her family that she never wanted this kind of terrible death, being maintained by machines. I told them that while I

25 respected their view, there was nothing intrinsically lethal about her situation. The kidney failure she had was just the kind for which the artificial kidney was most effective. While possibly a bit reassured, they were disappointed. Here was the head surgeon seemingly

30 determined to keep everybody alive, no matter what.

    When patients start to get very sick, they often seem to fall apart all at once. The reverse is also true. Within a few days, the patient's pacemaker could be removed and she awoke from her coma. About six

35 months later I was again in my office. The door opened and in walked a gloriously fit woman. After some cheery words of appreciation, the father and son asked to speak to me alone. As soon as the door closed, both men became quite tearful. All that came out was, "We

40 want you to know how wrong we were."

[1] Morphine is a powerful narcotic. It can cause death in large doses (amounts).

The second patient was an 85-year-old lady whose hair caught fire while she was smoking. She arrived with a deep burn; I knew it would surely be fatal. As a remarkable coincidence there was a seminar going on
45 at the time in medical ethics, given by the wife of an official of our university. She asked me if I had any sort of ethical problem I could bring up for discussion. I described the case and asked the students their opinion. After the discussion, I made a remark that was, in
50 retrospect, a serious mistake. I said, "I'll take the word back to the nurses about her and we will talk about it some more before we decide." The instructor and the students were shocked: "You mean this is a real patient?" The teacher of ethics was not accustomed to be-
55 ing challenged by reality. In any event, I went back and met with the nurses. A day or two later, when she was making no progress and was suffering terribly, we began to back off treatment. When she complained of pain, we gave her plenty of morphine. A great plenty.
60 Soon she died quietly and not in pain. As a reasonable physician, you had better move ahead and do what you would want done for you. And don't discuss it with the world first. There is a lesson here for everybody. Assisting people to leave this life requires strong judge-
65 ment and long experience to avoid its misuse.

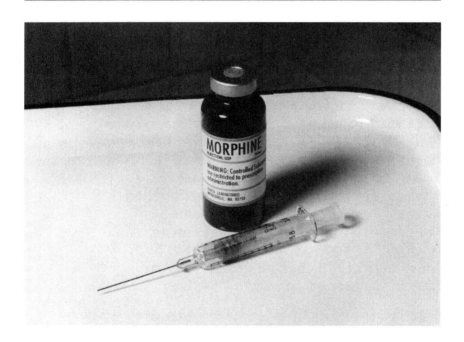

• A. Reading Overview: Main Idea, Details, and Summary

Read the passage again. As you read, underline what you think are the most important ideas in the reading. Then, in one or two sentences, write the main idea of the reading. *Use your own words.*

Main idea:

_____

_____

_____

Details:

Use the flowchart below to organize the information in the article. Refer back to the information you underlined in the passage as a guide. When you have finished, write a brief summary of the reading. *Use your own words.*

Matters of Life and Death

Summary:

_____

_____

_____

_____

• B. Statement Evaluation

Read the following statements. Then scan the article again quickly to find out if each sentence is **True (T), False (F),** or an **Inference (I).**

1. ___F___ The first patient discussed, who was formerly a nurse, died.

2. ___T___ The first patient's husband and son wanted the doctor to end her life.

3. ___T___ The instructor and students were very surprised that Dr. Moore was discussing a real patient.

4. ___I___ Dr. Moore gave the 85-year-old woman enough morphine so that she would die.

5. ___I___ Dr. Moore would probably choose assisted suicide if he should become terminally ill.

• C. Reading Analysis

Read each question carefully. Either circle the letter or number of the correct answer, or write your answer in the space provided.

1. Read lines 1–8.

    a. An **excerpt** is
        1. an example of an issue
        2. a part of a longer reading
        3. an introduction to a book

    b. **Doctors of our generation** refers to

        1. old doctors
        2. young doctors
        3. doctors about the same age as the author

    c. What does **this question** refer to?

    _____

    d. **My internship days** refers to

        1. the time when the author was younger
        2. a time in the recent past
        3. the time when the author was training as a doctor

2. Read lines 8–11: **"It was essential, not controversial."**

    a. What was essential?

    _____

    b. **Essential** means

        1. necessary
        2. medicine
        3. expensive

    c. **Controversial** refers to

        1. something people agree on
        2. something people argue about
        3. something people have to do

3. Read lines 19–21. **Rounds** refers to

    a. circular motions
    b. when doctors go around a hospital visiting their patients
    c. when a person is put on a breathing machine

4. Read lines 24–28. **"There was nothing intrinsically lethal about her situation"** means

   a. the woman's condition was fatal
   b. the woman's condition was not fatal

5. Read lines 31–36.

   a. What does **"the reverse is also true"** mean?

   _____

   b. Read lines 17–19 and lines 32–34. What is a **pacemaker?**

   _____

   c. How do you know?

   _____

6. Read lines 34–40. Who was **the gloriously fit woman?**

   _____

7. Read lines 41–43. **"I knew it would surely be fatal"** means

   a. the doctor thought the patient might live
   b. the doctor thought the patient might die
   c. the doctor knew the patient would die

8. Read lines 43–56.

   a. **In retrospect** means
      1. looking at something seriously
      2. looking sadly at something
      3. looking back at a past situation

   b. In line 55, **in any event** means

      1. anyway
      2. however
      3. in addition

9. Read lines 60–65. **"Don't discuss it with the world first"** means

   a. don't talk about your patients at seminars
   b. don't talk about your patients with nurses
   c. don't talk to many people about your patients

D. Dictionary Skills

Read the entry for each word, and consider the context of the sentence from the passage. Write the number of the definition that is appropriate for the context on the line next to the word. Write the entry number too when appropriate. Be prepared to explain your choice.

1. There was a seminar going on at the time in medical **ethics**, given by the wife of an official of our university.

   ethic: _____

   eth·ic \'e-thik\ *n* [ME *ethik,* fr. MF *ethique,* fr. L *ethice,* fr. Gk *ēthikē,* fr. *ēthikos*] (14c)   **1** *pl but sing or pl in constr* : the discipline dealing with what is good and bad and with moral duty and obligation   **2   a** : a set of moral principles or values   **b** : a theory or system of moral values ⟨the present-day materialistic ∼⟩   **c** *pl but sing or pl in constr* : the principles of conduct governing an individual or a group ⟨professional ∼s⟩   **d** : a guiding philosophy

2. The first patient had sustained a **fractured** pelvis in an automobile accident.

   fracture: _____

   ¹frac·ture \'frak-chər, -shər\ *n* [ME, fr. L *fractura,* fr. *fractus*] (15c)   **1** : the result of fracturing : BREAK   **2   a** : the act or process of breaking or the state of being broken; *esp* : the breaking of hard tissue (as bone)   **b** : the rupture (as by tearing) of soft tissue ⟨kidney ∼⟩   **3** : the general appearance of a freshly broken surface of a mineral
   ²fracture *vb* **frac·tured; frac·tur·ing** \-chə-riŋ, -shriŋ\ *vt* (1612)   **1   a** : to cause a fracture in : BREAK ⟨∼ a rib⟩   **b** : RUPTURE, TEAR   **2   a** : to damage or destroy as if by rupturing   **b** : to cause great disorder in   **c** : to break up : FRACTIONATE   **d** : to go beyond the limits of (as rules) : VIOLATE ⟨*fractured* the English language with malaprops —Goodman Ace⟩   ∼ *vi* : to undergo fracture

Pronunciation Guide

\ə\ abut   \ʰ\ kitten, F table   \ər\ further   \a\ ash   \ā\ ace   \ä\ mop, mar
\aů\ out   \ch\ chin   \e\ bet   \ē\ easy   \g\ go   \i\ hit   \ī\ ice   \j\ job
\ŋ\ sing   \ō\ go   \ȯ\ law   \ȯi\ boy   \th\ thin   \t̲h̲\ the   \ü\ loot   \ů\ foot
\y\ yet   \zh\ vision   \à, k̲, ⁿ, œ, œ̄, ɶ, ɶ̄, ʸ\

3. The patient's heartbeat was **maintained** with an electrical device (a pacemaker).

   The man and his son told me their wife and mother was obviously going to die; she had told her family that she never wanted this kind of terrible death, being **maintained** by machines.

maintain:

main·tain \mān-'tān, mən-\ *vt* [ME *mainteinen*, fr. OF *maintenir*, fr. ML *manutenēre*, fr. L *manu tenēre* to hold in the hand] (14c) **1** : to keep in an existing state (as of repair, efficiency, or validity) : preserve from failure or decline ⟨∼ machinery⟩ **2** : to sustain against opposition or danger : uphold and defend ⟨∼ a position⟩ **3** : to continue or persevere in : CARRY ON, KEEP UP ⟨couldn't ∼ his composure⟩ **4 a** : to support or provide for ⟨has a family to ∼⟩ **b** : SUSTAIN ⟨enough food to ∼ life⟩ **5** : to affirm in or as if in argument : ASSERT ⟨∼ed that the earth is flat⟩ — **main·tain·abil·i·ty** \-ˌtā-nə-'bi-lə-tē\ *n* — **main·tain·able** \-'tā-nə-bəl\ *adj* — **main·tain·er** *n*
syn MAINTAIN, ASSERT, DEFEND, VINDICATE, JUSTIFY mean to uphold as true, right, just, or reasonable. MAINTAIN stresses firmness of conviction ⟨steadfastly *maintained* his innocence⟩. ASSERT suggests determination to make others accept one's claim ⟨*asserted* her rights⟩. DEFEND implies maintaining in the face of attack or criticism ⟨*defended* his voting record⟩. VINDICATE implies successfully defending ⟨his success *vindicated* our faith in him⟩. JUSTIFY implies showing to be true, just, or valid by appeal to a standard or to precedent ⟨the action was used to *justify* military intervention⟩.

4. The first patient had **sustained** a fractured pelvis in an automobile accident.

sustain:

sus·tain \sə-'stān\ *vt* [ME *sustenen*, fr. OF *sustenir*, fr. L *sustinēre* to hold up, sustain, fr. *sub-*, *sus-* up + *tenēre* to hold — more at SUB-, THIN] (13c) **1** : to give support or relief to **2** : to supply with sustenance : NOURISH **3** : KEEP UP, PROLONG **4** : to support the weight of : PROP; *also* : to carry or withstand (a weight or pressure) **5** : to buoy up ⟨∼ed by hope⟩ **6 a** : to bear up under **b** : SUFFER, UNDERGO ⟨∼ed heavy losses⟩ **7 a** : to support as true, legal, or just **b** : to allow or admit as valid ⟨the court ∼ed the motion⟩ **8** : to support by adequate proof : CONFIRM ⟨testimony that ∼s our contention⟩ — **sus·tained·ly** \-'stā-nəd-lē, -'stānd-lē\ *adv* — **sus·tain·er** *n*

• E. Critical Thinking

Read each question carefully. Write your response in the space provided. Remember that there is no one correct answer. Your response depends on what **you** think.

1. Reread Dr. Quill's answer to the interviewer's fourth question. Consider his response with regard to Dr. Moore's experience in the medical ethics seminar. Do you think Dr. Moore and Dr. Quill would agree on the matter of debating the ethics of assisted suicide? Explain your answer.

   _____

   _____

   _____

2. What did the husband and the son of the former nurse want the doctor to do? Why were they disappointed?

   _____

   _____

   _____

3. When the father and son revisited him, Dr. Moore states that "both men became quite tearful." Why do you think they reacted this way?

   _____

   _____

   _____

4. Why did the doctors give the 85-year-old woman "plenty of morphine"? What does Dr. Moore mean by **"a great plenty"**?

   _____

   _____

   _____

5. In giving advice, Dr. Moore states, **"And don't discuss it with the world first."** What do you think **"it"** refers to? Why does Dr. Moore say not to discuss it with the world?

   _____

   _____

   _____

• Another Perspective

Should Doctors Be Allowed to Help Terminally Ill Patients Commit Suicide?

Health

1 **YES**

It would be a great comfort to people who face terminal illness to know they could get help to 5 die if their suffering became unbearable. All pain cannot be controlled, and it's arrogant for anybody to say that it can. Quality of life decisions are the sole 10 right of the individual.

It's nonsense to say that death shouldn't be part of a doctor's job—it already is. We all die. Death is a part of medicine. 15 One of a doctor's jobs is to write death certificates. So this idea of the doctor as superhealer is a load of nonsense. The fact is that it's not so easy to commit

NO

If it's a question of someone's wanting the right to die, I say jump off a building. But as soon as you bring in somebody else to help you, it changes the equation. Suicide is legally available to people in this country. Just don't ask a doctor to help you do it. That would violate the traditions of medicine and raise doubts about the role of the physician.

One of my worries is that people will be manipulated by a doctor's suggesting suicide. A lot of seriously ill people already feel they're a burden because they're costing their families

20 suicide on your own. It's very hard for decent citizens to get deadly drugs. Even if they do, there's the fear that the drugs won't work. There are hundreds
25 of dying people who couldn't lift their hand to their mouth with a cup of coffee, let alone a cup of drugs. They need assistance.

Of course, people who are
30 depressed or who feel they are a weight on their families should be counseled and helped to live. But you have to separate those instances from people who are
35 dying, whose bodies are giving up on them. If you think there is a cure around the corner for your malady, then please wait for it. That is your choice. But
40 sometimes a person realizes that her life is coming to an end, as in the case of my wife, whose doctor said, "There is nothing else we can do."

45 We're not talking about cases in which a depressed person will come to a doctor and ask to be killed. Under the law the Hemlock Society is trying to
50 get passed, the doctor must say no to depressed people. A candidate for assisted suicide has to be irreversibly, terminally, hopelessly ill and judged to be so by
55 two doctors.

money. It would be easy for a family to insinuate, "While we love you, Grandmother, and we're willing to spend all our money and not send the kids to college, wouldn't it be better if . . . ?" There is no coercion there, but you build on somebody's guilt. We'd have a whole new class of people considering suicide who hadn't thought about it before.

Then, too, I don't believe that you could successfully regulate this practice. The relationship between the doctor and the patient begins in confidentiality. If they decide together that they don't want anybody to know, there is no way the government can regulate it. The presumption is that physicians would only be helping people commit suicide after everything else had failed to end their suffering. But a lot of people won't want to be that far along. None of the proposed regulations take into account a person who is not suffering now, but who says, "I don't want to suffer in the future. Let me commit suicide now." I can imagine a doctor who would say, "Yes, we're going to make sure that you don't have to suffer at all."

Derek Humphry is the founder of the Hemlock Society and author of Final Exit, *a book advising terminally ill people on* how to commit suicide.

Daniel Callahan is a bioethicist and director of the Hastings Center, a medical ethics think tank in Briarcliff Manor, New York.

• Questions for "Should Doctors Be Allowed to Help Ill Patients Commit Suicide?"

1. Describe Derek Humphry's position on doctor-assisted suicide for

   a. terminally ill people

   _____

   _____

   b. depressed people

   _____

   _____

2. What do you think happened to Derek Humphry's wife? Why do you think so?

   _____

   _____

   _____

3. Describe Daniel Callahan's position on doctor-assisted suicide for terminally ill people.

   _____

   _____

   _____

4. What are some reasons that Daniel Callahan gives for his opinion?

   _____

   _____

   _____

• F. Follow-up Activities

1. Refer to the **Self-Evaluation of Reading Strategies** on pages 184–185. Think about the strategies you used to help yourself understand "Matters of Life and Death." Check off the strategies you used. Think about the strategies you didn't use, and try to apply them to help yourself understand the readings that follow.

2. Work with one or two classmates. Review the various perspectives given by the authors in this chapter. Whose perspective was included? Whose perspective was omitted? What perspectives might these excluded people have? Make a list of these people and their possible perspectives, and discuss them with the class.

3. a. Work in small groups of three or four students. Discuss the following case.

   "Martin" is a 40-year-old father of two young children. He was recently involved in a serious car accident and was critically injured. The doctors have declared him "brain dead," which means that his brain does not show any mental activity at all. He is being kept alive on a feeding tube and a respirator that breathes for him because he cannot breathe on his own. The doctors do not believe he will ever improve. However, he could be kept alive, but unconscious, on the machines indefinitely. The family must make an extremely difficult decision: Should they continue to keep Martin on these machines in the hospital, which is costing thousands of dollars a day, or should they allow him to die? Although Martin's family does not have a lot of money, they love him very much. What do you think they should do? What might be the consequences of the decision you think they should make?

   b. Form a medical ethics committee. Discuss all the class groups' decisions and their possible consequences. Then, as a class, decide what you think Martin's family should do.

   c. Think about how you came to your decision. What factors or values influenced your decision?

• G. Topics for Discussion and Writing

1. In the United States, some people write a "living will" before their death. A "living will" can prevent doctors from prolonging a person's life if he or she becomes seriously ill. For example, this means that the person may not want to be resuscitated if he or she stops breathing, or placed on a respirator or feeding tube if he cannot breathe or eat on his or her own. Would you want to write a "living will"? If not, why not? If so, under what conditions would you want to be allowed to die naturally? Write a composition explaining your answer.

2. What is your opinion on doctor-assisted suicide? Should it be legal? Should it be banned? Write a paragraph stating your opinion. Then discuss your opinion with your classmates.

3. **Write in your journal.** If someone you loved was terminally ill and wanted his or her doctor to perform an assisted suicide, would you approve? Would you encourage the doctor to agree to assist in the suicide? Explain your reasons.

Sales of Kidneys Prompt New Laws and Debate

• Prereading Preparation

Read the following article. Then complete the survey and answer the questions that follow.

Trading Flesh Around the Globe

Time

A ghoulish[1] notion: people so poor that they sell some of their body parts to survive. But for scores of brokers who buy and sell human organs in Asia, Latin America and Europe, that theme from a late-night horror movie is merely a matter of supply and demand. There are thousands more patients in need of kidneys, corneas, skin grafts and other human tissue than there are donors; therefore, big money can be made on a thriving black market in human flesh.

In India, the going rate for a kidney from a live donor is $1,500; for a cornea, $4,000; for a patch of skin, $50. Two centers of the thriving kidney trade are Bombay, where private clinics cater to Indians and a foreign clientele dominated by wealthy Arabs, and Madras, a center for patients from Malaysia, Singapore and Thailand. Renal patients in India and Pakistan who cannot find a relative to donate a kidney are permitted to buy newspaper advertisements offering living donors up to $4,300 for the organ. Mohammad Aqeel, a poor Karachi tailor who recently sold one of his kidneys for $2,600, said he needed the money "for the marriage of two daughters and paying off of debts."

---

[1] *Ghoulish* is the adjective form of *ghoul*, which refers to a legendary evil creature that robs graves and eats the dead. It is an extremely negative word.

Reprinted with permission from *Time* magazine, "The Gift of Life," Lance Morrow, June 17, 1991.

In India, Africa, Latin America, and Eastern Europe, young people advertise organs for sale, sometimes to pay for college educations. In Hong Kong a businessman named Tsui Fung circulated a letter to doctors in March offering to serve as middleman between patients seeking the kidney transplants and a Chinese military hospital in Nanjing that performs the operation. The letter said the kidneys would come from live "volunteers," implying that they would be paid donors. The fee for the kidney, the operation and round-trip airfare: $12,800.

1. Work with your classmates in small groups. Answer the following survey about selling organs. When you are finished, compile the class's answers on the blackboard.

Would you sell:	Student 1	Student 2	Student 3	Student 4
one of your kidneys?	Yes/No	Yes/No	Yes/No	Yes/No
one of your corneas?	Yes/No	Yes/No	Yes/No	Yes/No
a patch of your skin?	Yes/No	Yes/No	Yes/No	Yes/No
a lobe from your lung?	Yes/No	Yes/No	Yes/No	Yes/No

2. Look at the results of your class survey. What are the conditions under which your classmates would sell their organs? Ask the students who answered *yes* to complete the following statement:

I would sell _____ for the following

reasons: _____ .

3. Read the title of this article. What new laws and what debate do you think the sale of kidneys has prompted?

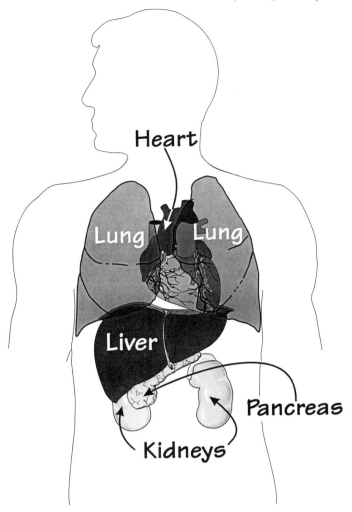

Sales of Kidneys Prompt New Laws and Debate

by Terry Trucco
The New York Times

1   Last summer Colin Benton died after receiving a kidney transplant at a private London hospital. Several months later, however, his case made headlines throughout Britain when his widow disclosed that her
5 husband's kidney transplant had come from a Turkish citizen who was paid $3,300 to fly to Britain and donate the organ. The donor said he had decided to sell his kidney to pay for medical treatment for his daughter. Concern in Britain over issues raised in the case re-
10 sulted in a law passed on July 28, 1989 in Parliament banning the sale of human organs for transplant.

The same concerns and those over loopholes in the transplant laws in some other nations led the World Health Organization to condemn the practice recently.
15 In a resolution in May, the organization asked member nations to take appropriate measures, including legislation, to prohibit trafficking in human organs.

But as Britain was moving to make the sale of human organs unlawful, as it is in the United States, ethi-
20 cists and policy analysts in the United States were beginning to suggest that paying donors, or their estates, may be an effective way to increase the supply of organs available for transplant.

The idea of organs for sale "is creeping into health
25 care discussions," Joel L. Swerdlow said in a recent report for the Annenberg Washington Program, a public policy research group affiliated with Northwestern University in Evanston, Illinois. "The altruistic 'gift relationship' may be inadequate as a motivator and an
30 anachronism in medicine today, he wrote. "If paying seems wrong, it may nevertheless be preferable to accepting the suffering and death of patients who cannot otherwise obtain transplants."

Doctors, lawyers and health authorities say the sale
35 of organs by impoverished donors is a growing phenomenon. Because it is possible to live with just one kidney and because demand for the organs is so high, kidneys are among the most popular organs for commercial transactions. People have sold their own blood for years.
40 The new British law makes it a criminal offense to give or receive money for supplying organs of either a living or dead person. It also prohibits acting as a broker in such an arrangement, advertising for organs for payment or transplanting an organ from a live donor
45 not closely related to the recipient.

A new computerized nationwide registry, which records all transplants from both live donors and cadavers, will be used to help enforce the law. Punishment for breaking the law is either a $3,300 fine or
50 three months in prison. Doctors convicted under the law could lose their right to practice medicine.

The health organization's resolution calls for compiling information on organ trafficking laws in member countries and publicizing the findings. At least 20
55 other countries, including the United States, Canada

and most of Western Europe, already have laws or policies prohibiting the sale of human organs.

Britain has had a transplant law since the 1961 Human Tissue Act, which deemed it unethical for a practi
60 tioner to traffic in human organs. But the new law is
believed to be the world's first legislation aimed exclusively at the commercial organ transactions. The British
law applies only to transplants performed in the
nation's private hospitals and not to those overseen by
65 the government-supported National Health Service,
which provides free medical care for British citizens.
The service, which has not used paid donors, gets first
pick of all kidneys available for transplant in the nation. At present, about 1,600 transplants are performed
70 each year, with a waiting list of about 3,600 patients.

But as in the United States, many patients from
countries without high-quality kidney care come to
Britain each year to undergo transplants in private hospitals. These hospitals rely on cadaver kidneys or live
75 donor transplants from relatives of patients.

In the past, doctors simply questioned foreign donors to make certain they were related to recipients, but
most admit the system was hardly foolproof. Often doctors could not communicate with patients who did not
80 speak English. A doctor involved in the Benton case said
he attempted to find out if the donor had been paid by
waving a 5-pound note at him. "A number of us were
duped by patients with forged medical referrals and
documents saying they were relatives," said Maurice
85 Slapak, director of a hospital transplant unit in Britain.

Despite the speed and ease with which the British
transplant law was passed, it remains controversial. In a
letter to The Times of London, Royden Harrison, professor emeritus at Warwick University, wrote: "What pos
90 sible objection can there be if one person, of their own
free will, should sell their kidney to someone else? The
seller is able to indulge in a few of the good things in
life. The buyer may well be paying to survive." Sir
Michael McNair Wilson, a member of Parliament who is
95 on a waiting list for a new kidney, has argued that selling a kidney is like women in the nineteenth century
selling their hair. "As someone waiting to receive a
transplant, I would only like to feel that the organ I am
given is a gift from someone," he said. "But while there

100 is a shortage of kidneys, I do not see why it is wrong for
you to do what you will with your body."

"If it takes $25,000 to $30,000 annually to keep
someone alive on an artificial kidney machine," John
M. Newman wrote in the Annenberg Program report,
105 "government payment of, for example, $5,000 for
transplantable cadaver kidneys (even with the cost of
transportation), would still make successful kidney
transplantation cost effective." Dr. Newman, a kidney
transplant recipient, is a director of the American As-
110 sociation of Kidney Patients. "This is not to suggest
that a monetary value can be placed on human life or
on life-saving organs," he added. "This does suggest,
however, that a monetary 'thank you' from the Federal
Government could stimulate increases in organ and tis-
115 sue availability for transplantation and research."

There is concern that the new law could scare off
suitable donors and add to the shortage of kidneys by
somehow creating the impression that all donations are
improper. A report by the National Kidney Research
120 Fund said there had been a dramatic fall in the number
of kidney donations earlier this year following the kid-
ney-for-sale controversy. "There have effectively been at
least 100 fewer transplant operations this year, and that
means 100 people may have died because of the unfa-
125 vorable publicity," the organization said in a statement.

Some opponents of the law simply think that it is
addressing the wrong health issue. Elizabeth Ward,
founder of the British Kidney Patients Association, supports legislation that would make organ donation auto-
130 matic upon death. Those who choose not to donate
would have to make a formal request. But Belgium began such a program several years ago, and it has had
little effect. Doctors are reluctant to use the law. Doctors still ask next of kin for permission to remove or-
135 gans. It's a moral issue. Nevertheless, many in the
medical profession think the law was needed.

"If we take the very extreme view, people in desperate circumstances might be prepared to martyr themselves, selling their hearts to save their families," said
140 Ross Taylor, director of transplant surgery at the Royal
Victoria Infirmary in Newcastle Upon Tyne and president of the British Transplantation Society. Mr. Taylor
also criticized those tempted to sell their organs for

145 frivolous reasons. "I have met people prepared to sell their kidneys to buy Porsches or to take a girlfriend on a holiday."

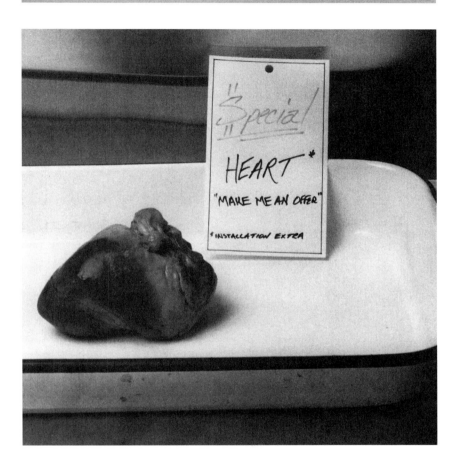

• A. Reading Overview: Main Idea, Details, and Summary

Read the passage again. As you read, underline what you think are the most important ideas in the reading. Then, in one or two sentences, write the main idea of the reading. *Use your own words.*

Main idea:

_____

_____

_____

Details:

Use the outline below to organize the information in the article. Refer back to the information you underlined in the passage as a guide. When you have finished, write a brief summary of the reading. *Use your own words.*

Sales of Kidneys Prompt New Laws and Debate

	Britain	World Health Organization	United States	Belgium
Laws about organ donation				
Opinions about sales of organs				✕
Arguments in favor of a law prohibiting the sale of organs	1. 2. 3. 4.			
Arguments against a law prohibiting the sale of organs	1. 2.			

Summary:

_____

_____

_____

• B. Statement Evaluation

Read the following statements. Then scan the article again quickly to find out if each sentence is **True (T), False (F),** or **Not Mentioned (NM)** in the article.

1. _____ In Britain it is legal to sell organs.

2. _____ The World Health Organization supports the sale of organs for transplants.

3. _____ In the United States, it is unlawful to sell organs.

4. _____ Some policy analysts in the United States think that paying donors may increase the number of organ transplants.

5. _____ Most of Asia already has laws prohibiting the sale of human organs.

6. _____ In Britain, organ donation is automatic when someone dies.

7. _____ Dr. John M. Newman paid the person who donated a kidney to him.

8. _____ In Belgium, organ donation is automatic when someone dies.

• C. Reading Analysis

Read each question carefully. Either circle the letter or number of the correct answer, or write your answer in the space provided.

1. Read lines 1–11.

    a. Who is the **donor?**
       1. the person who receives the organ
       2. the person who gives the organ

    b. In the sentence **"Concern in Britain over issues raised in the case...,"** what is one of the **issues** in this **case?**

       1. Colin Benton's kidney donor was paid $3,300.
       2. Colin Benton died after his kidney transplant.

2. Read lines 12–17.

    a. What does **the practice** refer to?

    _____

    b. **To prohibit trafficking in human organs** means

       1. to allow the buying and selling of human organs
       2. to forbid the buying and selling of human organs
       3. to control the buying and selling of human organs

3. Read lines 34–39. **Impoverished donors** are

    a. healthy
    b. important
    c. poor

4. Read lines 58–70.

    a. In **"The service . . . gets first pick . . . ,"** what is **the service?**

    _____

    b. **"Gets first pick"** means the service

       1. has first choice of the available kidneys
       2. can decide which hospital gets kidneys

5. Read lines 71–75.

    a. What are **live donors** and **cadavers?**

       1. opposites
       2. synonyms

b. What is a **cadaver?**

   1. a donor
   2. an organ
   3. a dead body

6. Read lines 102–108. **"$5,000 for transplantable cadaver kidneys . . . would still make successful kidney transplantation cost effective"** means

   a. it's less expensive to pay a donor for a kidney than it is to keep someone alive on an artificial kidney machine
   b. it's less expensive to keep someone alive on an artificial kidney machine than it is to pay a donor for a kidney

7. Read lines 126–136. Who are **next of kin?**

   a. lawyers
   b. other doctors
   c. family members

8. Read lines 137–146.

   a. What does **to martyr themselves** mean?

      1. to die
      2. to undergo an operation
      3. to put themselves in danger

   b. What are examples of **frivolous reasons** why people might sell their organs?

   _____

   c. What does **frivolous** mean?

      1. exciting; fun
      2. minor; trivial
      3. expensive; costly

• D. Dictionary Skills

Read the entry for each word, and consider the context of the sentence from the passage. Write the definition that is appropriate for the context in the line next to the word. Write the entry number too when appropriate. Be prepared to explain your choice.

1. Some opponents of the British transplant law think that it **addresses** the wrong health issue.

   address: _____

   ad·dress \ə-'dres, a- *also* 'a-,dres\ *vb* [ME *adressen,* fr. MF *adresser,* fr. *a-* (fr. L *ad-*) + *dresser* to arrange — more at DRESS] *vt* (14c) **1** *archaic* **a :** DIRECT, AIM **b :** to direct to go : SEND **2** **a :** to direct the efforts or attention of (oneself) ⟨will ∼ himself to the problem⟩ **b :** to deal with : TREAT ⟨intrigued by the chance to ∼ important issues —I. L. Horowitz⟩ **3** *archaic* : to make ready; *esp* : DRESS **4** **a :** to communicate directly ⟨∼es his thanks to his host⟩ **b :** to speak or write directly to; *esp* : to deliver a formal speech to **5** **a :** to mark directions for delivery on ⟨∼ a letter⟩ **b :** to consign to the care of another (as an agent or factor) **6 :** to greet by a prescribed form **7 :** to adjust the club preparatory to hitting (a golf ball) **8 :** to identify (as a peripheral or memory location) by an address or a name for information transfer ∼ *vi, obs* : to direct one's speech or attentions — **ad·dress·er** *n*

2. Colin Benton's case made headlines when his widow **disclosed** that his kidney transplant had come from a Turkish citizen.

   disclose: _____

   dis·close \dis-'klōz\ *vt* [ME, fr. MF *desclos-,* stem of *desclore* to disclose, fr. ML *disclaudere* to open, fr. L *dis-* + *claudere* to close — more at CLOSE] (14c) **1** *obs* : to open up **2** **a :** to expose to view **b** *archaic* : HATCH **c :** to make known or public ⟨demands that politicians ∼ the sources of their income⟩ *syn* see REVEAL — **dis·clos·er** *n*

3. a. The World Health Organization recently condemned the **practice** of selling human organs for transplant.

   b. Doctors who are convicted under the British transplant law may lose their medical license and their **practice**.

   practice: _(a)_____   (b)_____

   practice *also* **practise** *n* (15c) **1** **a :** actual performance or application ⟨ready to carry out in ∼ what they advocated in principle⟩ **b :** a repeated or customary action ⟨had this irritating ∼⟩ **c :** the usual way of doing something ⟨local ∼s⟩ **d :** the form, manner, and order of conducting legal suits and prosecutions **2** **a :** systematic exercise for proficiency ⟨∼ makes perfect⟩ **b :** the condition of being proficient through systematic exercise ⟨get in ∼⟩ **3** **a :** the continuous exercise of a profession **b :** a professional business; *esp* : one constituting an incorporeal property *syn* see HABIT

4. The World Health Organization wants member nations to create legislation that would make it illegal to **traffic in** human organs. In fact, Britain's transplant law deems it unethical for a practitioner to **traffic in** any human organs.

traffic in: _____

¹traf·fic \'tra-fik\ *n, often attrib* [MF *trafique,* fr. OIt *traffico,* fr. *trafficare* to traffic] (1506) **1 a :** import and export trade **b :** the business of bartering or buying and selling **c :** illegal or disreputable usu. commercial activity ⟨the drug ∼⟩ **2 a :** communication or dealings esp. between individuals or groups **b :** EXCHANGE ⟨a lively ∼ in ideas —F. L. Allen⟩ **3** *archaic* : WARES, GOODS **4 a :** the movement (as of vehicles or pedestrians) through an area or along a route **b :** the vehicles, pedestrians, ships, or planes moving along a route **c :** the information or signals transmitted over a communications system : MESSAGES **5 a :** the passengers or cargo carried by a transportation system **b :** the business of transporting passengers or freight **6 :** the volume of customers visiting a business establishment *syn* see BUSINESS — **the traffic will bear :** existing conditions will allow or permit ⟨charge what *the traffic will bear*⟩
²traffic *vb* **traf·ficked; traf·fick·ing** *vi* (1540) **:** to carry on traffic ∼ *vt* **1 :** to travel over ⟨heavily *trafficked* highways⟩ **2 :** TRADE, BARTER — **traf·fick·er** *n*

Pronunciation Guide

\ə\ abut \ʾ\ kitten, F table \ər\ **further** \a\ **ash** \ā\ **ace** \ä\ **mop, mar**
\au̇\ **out** \ch\ **chin** \e\ **bet** \ē\ **easy** \g\ **go** \i\ **hit** \ī\ **ice** \j\ **job**
\ŋ\ **sing** \ō\ **go** \ȯ\ **law** \ȯi\ **boy** \th\ **thin** \th̲\ **the** \ü\ **loot** \u̇\ **foot**
\y\ **yet** \zh\ **vision** \à, k̲,ⁿ, œ, ōe, ue, ūe, ʸ\

• E. Critical Thinking

Read each question carefully. Write your response in the space provided. Remember that there is no one correct answer. Your response depends on what **you** think.

1. Does the author present the information in the article subjectively or objectively? Explain the reasons for your answer.

   _____

   _____

2. How do you think Terry Trucco, the journalist who wrote the kidney sales article, feels about this issue? What makes you think this?

   _____

   _____

3. Refer to the case of Colin Benton.

   a. Why did Mrs. Benton's disclosure make headlines throughout Britain?

   _____

   _____

   b. What issues do you think were raised as a result of this case?

   _____

   _____

4. Compare the growing attitude in the United States to the new legislation in Britain. How are the policies of the two countries changing?

   _____

   _____

5. Both Sir Michael McNair Wilson and Dr. John M. Newman are in favor of the sale of human organs for transplants. What do you think might be some reasons for their opinion?

   _____

   _____

   _____

6. Sir Michael McNair Wilson has argued that selling a kidney is like women in the nineteenth century selling their hair. Do you think this is a reasonable comparison? Explain your answer.

_____

_____

_____

7. Elizabeth Ward suggests that organ donation should be made automatic upon death unless the individual specifically requests otherwise. Why does she think this is a better approach to the issue of organ donations than Britain's new law is?

_____

_____

_____

• F. Follow-up Activities

1. Refer to the **Self-Evaluation of Reading Strategies** on pages 184–185. Think about the strategies you used to help yourself understand "Sales of Kidneys Prompt New Laws and Debate." Check off the strategies you used. Think about the strategies you didn't use, and try to apply them to help yourself understand the readings that follow.

2. Look at the following chart carefully, then answer the related questions.

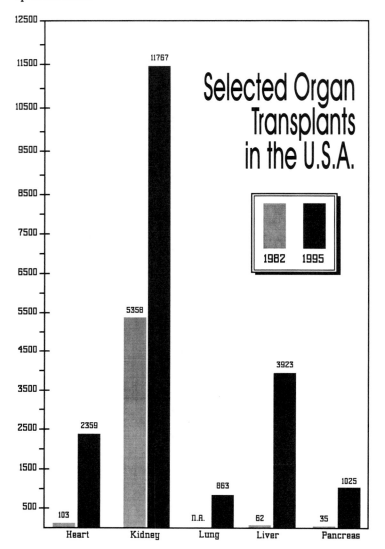

a. What does this graph compare?

_____

b. 1. In 1982, what type of organ transplant was most frequent?

_____

2. In 1995, what type of organ transplant was most frequent?

_____

3. Based on what you read in the article, what is the reason this organ is transplanted most frequently?

_____

c. 1. Which organ transplant operation increased the most in absolute numbers between 1982 and 1995?

_____

2. Which organ transplant operation showed the highest percentage of increase between 1982 and 1995?

_____

3. a. Below is a list of nine people who need heart transplants. Working alone, place these people in order of priority for a transplant. What factors (e.g., age, sex) should determine which patients receive priority?

b. Work in a group of three or four students. Your group is a panel of medical experts at a leading hospital in a large city. Your group must decide on the order in which to place these patients on the list to receive an organ. Discuss your individual decisions, then negotiate a single list of people in the order they will be placed on the waiting list.

Your Order	Your Group's Order	Sex	Age	Occupation	Personal Information	Length of Time Already Waiting
		F	36	housewife	3 children	12 months
		M	6	first grader	—	18 months
		M	71	heart surgeon	2 children, 3 grandchildren	9 months
		M	40	truck driver	widowed, 1 child	9 months
		F	24	kindergarten teacher	single, 2 siblings	12 months
		F	15	high school student	5 siblings	18 months
		F	47	cancer specialist	divorced, no children	12 months
		F	39	ESL teacher	married, 3 children	6 months
		M	52	banker	married, 1 child	10 months

• G. Topics for Discussion and Writing

1. In the United States, it is illegal to sell or buy organs. Do you think that governments have the right or the responsibility to make laws controlling the sale of organs? What are your reasons? Should this be a legal issue or a moral issue? Do you think it is wrong to buy or sell organs? Why or why not? Discuss your opinion with your classmates.

2. In Belgium, when a person dies, his or her organs are automatically donated unless that person had formally requested not to donate before he or she died. Do you think this is a good program? Would you want to donate your organs after your death? Why or why not? Write a paragraph explaining your answer.

3. Do you think the sale of organs from live donors will continue to be considered a moral issue, or will people come to see their nonvital organs as "investments" to be sold in time of economic need? If they do, does the government have the right to prevent people from selling their organs? Why or why not? If an individual wants to sell an organ in order to make money, does a surgeon have the right and/or the responsibility to refuse to perform the operation? Write a composition explaining your opinions.

4. Look back at the organ transplant chart on page 162. What do you think may be some reasons for the great increase in transplants in general? Discuss these reasons with your classmates.

5. **Write in your journal.** Would you volunteer as a living organ donor? If so, under what circumstances would you do so? If not, why not?

The Gift of Life: When One Body Can Save Another

• **Prereading Preparation**

1. Read the title of this article. Discuss it with a classmate. What do you think this reading will be about?

2. Read the following paragraphs about organ transplants. Then work with a partner to answer the questions.

> A doctor's new dilemma: two weeks ago, Ronald Busuttil, director of UCLA's liver-transplant program, heard that a liver, just the right size and blood type, was suddenly available for a man who had been waiting for a transplant. The patient, severely ill but not on the verge of death, was being readied for the procedure when the phone rang. A five-year-old girl who had previously been given a transplant had suffered a catastrophe. Her liver had stopped functioning. Busuttil had to make a decision. "I had two desperately ill patients," he says, but the choice was clear. Without an immediate transplant, "the little girl certainly would have died."

a. What was the doctor's dilemma?

_____

b. Describe each patient's condition:

The man's: _____

The little girl's: _____

c. What did the doctor decide to do?

_____

_____

d. Do you agree with his decision? Why or why not?

In the world of advanced medical technology, the uses of living tissue have become very suddenly more complex and problematic. A newly born infant suffering from the fatal congenital malformation known as anencephaly will surely die within a few days of birth. Anencephaly means a partial or complete absence of the cerebrum, cerebellum and flat bones of the skull. Such babies could be an invaluable source for organs and tissues for other needy infants. Is that sort of "harvesting" all right?

a. Is an anencephalic infant healthy? Why or why not?

_____

b. What will happen to such an infant?

_____

c. What is the ethical dilemma in this case?

_____

d. What is your opinion on this matter? In other words, *"Is that sort of 'harvesting' all right?"*

_____

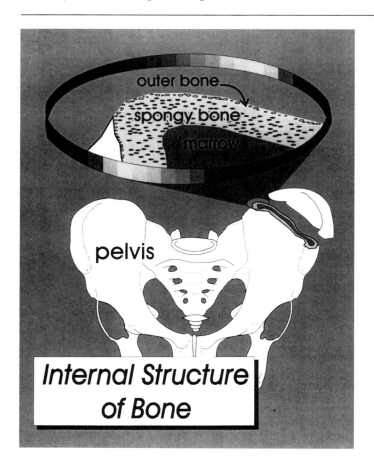

Internal Structure of Bone

The Gift of Life: When One Body Can Save Another

by Lance Morrow
Time

1   Now the long quest was ending. A 14-month-old girl
named Marissa Ayala lay anesthetized upon an operating table in the City of Hope National Medical Center in
Duarte, Calif. A surgeon inserted a one-inch-long
5   needle into the baby's hip and slowly began to draw
marrow. In 20 minutes, they removed about a cup of
the viscous red liquid.
       The medical team then rushed the marrow to a hos-
pital room where Marissa's 19-year-old sister Anissa
10   lay waiting. Through a Hickman catheter inserted in
the chest, the doctor began feeding the baby's marrow
into Anissa's veins. The marrow needed only to be
dripped into the girl's bloodstream. There the healthy
marrow cells began to find their way to the bones.
15   Done. If all goes well, if rejection does not occur or
a major infection set in, the marrow will do the work. It
will give life to the older sister, who otherwise would
have died of chronic myelogenous leukemia. Doctors
rate the chance of success at 70%.
20   The Ayala family had launched itself upon a se-
quence of nervy, life-or-death adventures to arrive at
the denouement last week. Anissa's leukemia was diagnosed three years ago. In such cases, the patient usually dies within five years unless she receives a marrow
25   transplant. Abe and Mary Ayala, who own a speedom-
eter-repair business, began a nationwide search for a
donor whose marrow would be a close match for
Anissa's. The search, surrounded by much poignant
publicity, failed.
30   The Ayalas did not passively accept their daughter's
fate. They knew from their doctors that the best hope
for Anissa lay in a marrow transplant from a sibling,
but the marrow of her only brother, Airon, was incompatible. Her life, it seemed, could depend on a sibling
35   who did not yet exist.
       First, Abe had to have his vasectomy surgically re-
versed, a procedure with a success rate of just 40%.
That done, Mary Ayala ventured to become pregnant at

the age of 43. The odds were one in four that the baby's
40 bone marrow would match her sister's. In April 1990
Mary bore a daughter, Marissa. Fetal stem cells were ex-
tracted from the umbilical cord and frozen for use
along with the marrow in last week's transplant. Then
everyone waited for the optimum moment—the baby
45 had to grow old enough and strong enough to donate
safely even while her older sister's time was waning.

Twelve days before the operation, Anissa began receiving intensive doses of radiation and chemotherapy
to kill her diseased bone marrow. As a result, she is
50 losing her hair. Her blood count is plummeting. Her
immune system has gone out of business. But in two to
four weeks, the new cells should take over and start
their work of giving Anissa a new life.

The drama of the Ayalas—making the baby, against
55 such long odds, to save the older daughter—seemed to
many to be a miracle. To others, it was profoundly, if
sometimes obscurely, troubling. What disturbed was the
spectacle of a baby being brought in to the world . . . to
serve as a means, a biological resupply vehicle. The
60 baby did not consent to be used. The parents created
the new life, then used that life for their own purposes,
however noble. Would the baby have agreed to the
transplant if she had been able to make the choice?

People wanting a baby have many reasons—reasons
65 frivolous, sentimental, practical, emotional, biological.
Farm families need children to work the fields. In
much of the world, children are social security for old
age. They are vanity items for many people, an extension of ego. Or a sometimes desperate measure to try
70 to save a marriage that is failing. Says Dr. Rudolf
Brutoco, Marissa Ayala's pediatrician: "Does it make
sense to conceive a child so that little Johnny can have
a sister, while it is not acceptable to conceive the same
child so that Johnny can live?" In American society,
75 procreation is a personal matter. Crack addicts or convicted child abusers are free to have children.

Considered on the family's own terms, their behavior is hard to fault. The first duty of parents is to protect their children. The Ayalas say they never
80 considered aborting the fetus if its marrow did not
match Anissa's. They will cherish both daughters in the
context of a miracle that allowed the older to live on
and the younger to be born.

But their case resonated with meanings and dilem-
85 mas larger than itself. The case opened out upon a
prospect of medical-technological possibility and danger. In the past it was mostly cadavers from which
transplant organs were "harvested." Today, as with the
Ayalas, life is being tapped to save life.[1]
90   Beyond the Ayala case, the ethics can become trickier.
What if a couple conceives a baby in order to obtain
matching marrow for another child; and what if amnio-
centesis shows that the tissue of the fetus is not compatible for transplant? Does the couple abort the fetus and
95 then try again? Says Dr. Norman Fost, a pediatrician and
ethicist at the University of Wisconsin: "If you believe
that a woman is entitled to terminate a pregnancy for any
reason at all, then it doesn't seem to me to make it any
worse to terminate a pregnancy for this reason." But
100 abortions are normally performed to end accidental preg-
nancies. What is the morality of ending a pregnancy that
was very deliberately undertaken in the first place?
        Transplant technology is developing so rapidly that
new practices are outpacing society's ability to explore
105 their moral implications. The first kidney transplants
were performed over 35 years ago and were greeted as
the brave new world: an amazing novelty. Today the
transplant is part of the culture—conceptually dazzling,
familiar in a weird way, but morally unassimilated. The
110 number of organ transplants exceeds 15,000 a year and
is growing at an annual clip of 15%. The variety of pro-
cedures is also expanding as surgeons experiment with
transplanting parts of the pancreas, the lung and other
organs. As of last week, 23,276 people were on the wait-
115 ing list of the United Network for Organ Sharing, a national registry and tracking service.
        A dire shortage of organs for these patients helps
make the world of transplants an inherently bizarre
one. Seat-belt and motorcycle-helmet laws are bad
120 news for those waiting for a donor. The laws reduce fa-
talities and therefore reduce available cadavers.
        Most organs come from cadavers, but the number
of living donors is rising. There were 1,788 last year,
up 15% from 1989. Of these, 1,773 provided kidneys,
125 nine provided portions of livers. Six of the living do-

---

[1] Postscript: The transplant operation was successful. Anissa survived and
Marissa suffered no adverse effects from the procedure.

nors gave their hearts away. How? They were patients who needed heart-lung transplant packages. To make way for the new heart, they gave up the old one; doctors call it the "domino practice."

130   In 1972 Dr. Thomas Starzl, the renowned Pittsburgh surgeon who pioneered liver transplants, stopped performing live-donor transplants of any kind. He explained why in a speech in 1987: "The death of a single well-motivated and completely healthy living donor al-

135 most stops the clock worldwide. The most compelling argument against living donation is that it is not completely safe for the donor." Starzl said he knew of 20 donors who had died, though other doctors regard this number as miraculously low, since there have been

140 more that 100,000 live-donor transplants.

There will never be enough cadaver organs to fill the growing needs of people dying from organ or tissue failure. This places higher and higher importance, and risk, on living relatives who might serve as do-

145 nors. Organs that are either redundant (one of a pair of kidneys) or regenerative (bone marrow) become more and more attractive. Transplants become a matter of high-stakes risk-calculation for the donor as well as the recipient and the intense emotions involved some-

150 times have people playing long shots.

Federal law now prohibits any compensation for organs in the United States. In China and India, there is a brisk trade in such organs as kidneys. Will the day come when Americans have a similar marketplace for organs? Turning the body into a commodity might in fact make families less willing to donate organs.

• A. Reading Overview: Main Idea, Details, and Summary

Read the passage again. As you read, underline what you think are the most important ideas in the reading. Then, in one or two sentences, write the main idea of the reading. *Use your own words.*

Main idea:

_____

_____

_____

Details:

Use the flowchart below to organize the information in the reading. Refer back to the information you underlined in the passage as a guide. When you have finished, write a brief summary of the reading. *Use your own words.*

The Gift of Life: When One Body Can Save Another

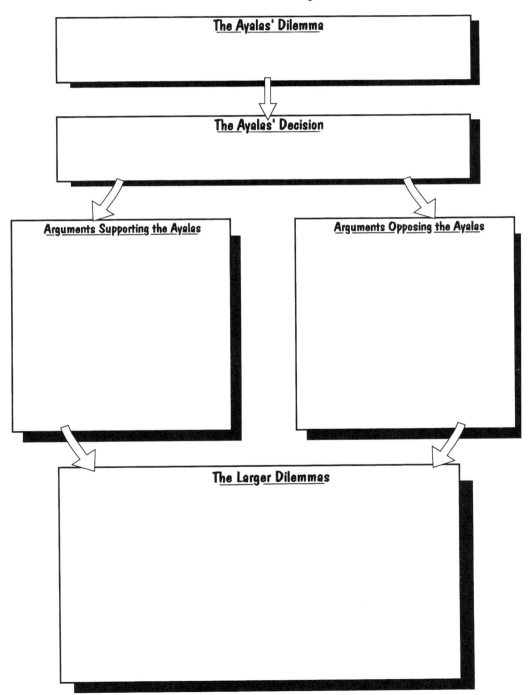

The Ayalas' Dilemma

The Ayalas' Decision

Arguments Supporting the Ayalas

Arguments Opposing the Ayalas

The Larger Dilemmas

Summary:

_____

_____

_____

_____

• B. Statement Evaluation

Read the following statements. Then scan the article again quickly to find out if each sentence is **True (T), False (F),** or an **Inference (I).**

1. _____ The bone marrow was taken from 19-year-old Anissa and given to 14-month-old Marissa.

2. _____ The older sister has a very serious disease.

3. _____ Marissa was born before Anissa became sick with leukemia.

4. _____ Dr. Rudolf Brutoco agreed with the Ayalas' decision to conceive a child in the hopes of saving Anissa.

5. _____ Dr. Norman Fost believes that the ethics of terminating a pregnancy is the same no matter what the reason.

6. _____ Living donors have given their hearts away.

7. _____ Dr. Thomas Starzl worries that an organ recipient may die as a result of the transplant operation.

• C. Reading Analysis

Read each question carefully. Either circle the letter or number of the correct answer, or write your answer in the space provided.

1. Read lines 8–14. A **catheter** is

   a. a type of medicine
   b. a thin plastic tube
   c. a small hole

2. Read lines 15–19. **"If all goes well"** means

   a. if the procedure works correctly
   b. if the sister dies
   c. if rejection occurs

3. Read lines 20–29.

   a. **Denouement** means

      1. problem
      2. solution
      3. hospital

   b. What does **in such cases** refer to?

   _____

4. Read lines 30–35.

   a. What was **their daughter's fate?**
      1. She would be sick for a long time.
      2. She would die within five years.
      3. She would receive marrow from a stranger.

   b. **"The marrow of her only brother . . . was incompatible"** means

      1. the marrow of Airon and Anissa was the same
      2. the marrow of Airon and Anissa was different

   c. **A sibling who did not yet exist** is a sibling who

      1. has not been conceived yet
      2. has already been born
      3. is not yet old enough

5. Read lines 39–46.

   a. When is the **optimum moment?**

   _____

   _____

   b. **Optimum** means

      1. best
      2. worst
      3. after one year

6. Read lines 54–63. In this paragraph, what word is a synonym of **consent?**

   _____

7. Read lines 64–76. What is **procreation?**

   a. having children
   b. taking drugs
   c. making a choice

8. Read lines 90–102. To have an **abortion** means to

   a. become pregnant
   b. terminate a pregnancy
   c. continue a pregnancy

9. Read lines 117–121.

   a. What are **seat-belt and motorcycle-helmet laws?**

   _____

   b. Why are these laws **"bad news for those waiting for a donor"?**

   _____

   _____

10. Read lines 130–140.

   a. **"The death of a . . . completely healthy living donor almost stops the clock worldwide"** means that the death of a healthy living donor

      1. discourages other healthy people from donating an organ
      2. discourages doctors from performing transplant operations using healthy living donors
      3. both 1 and 2

   b. **Compelling** means

      1. convincing
      2. healthy
      3. interesting

11. Read lines 151–156. **Prohibits any compensation** means

   a. you cannot receive money for donating an organ
   b. you cannot donate an organ from a cadaver
   c. you cannot donate an organ from a living donor

• D. Dictionary Skills

Read the entry for each word, and consider the context of the sentence from the passage. Write the definition that is appropriate for the context on the line next to the word. Write the entry number too when appropriate. Be prepared to explain your choice.

1. There will never be enough cadaver organs to fill the growing needs of people dying from organ or tissue **failure**.

   failure: _____

   fail·ure \'fā(ə)l-yər\ *n* [alter. of earlier *failer*, fr. AF, fr. OF *faillir* to fail] (1643) **1 a :** omission of occurrence or performance; *specif* : a failing to perform a duty or expected action **b :** a state of inability to perform a normal function ⟨kidney ∼⟩ — compare HEART FAILURE **c** : a fracturing or giving way under stress ⟨structural ∼⟩ **2 a :** lack of success **b :** a failing in business : BANKRUPTCY **3 a :** a falling short : DEFICIENCY ⟨a crop ∼⟩ **b :** DETERIORATION, DECAY **4 :** one that has failed

2. Considered on the family's own terms, the Ayalas' behavior (conceiving a baby to save their daughter) is hard to **fault**.

   fault: _____

   fault *vi* (15c) **1 :** to commit a fault : ERR **2 :** to fracture so as to produce a geologic fault ∼ *vt* **1 :** to find a fault in ⟨easy to praise this book and to ∼ it —H. G. Roepke⟩ **2 :** to produce a geologic fault in **3 :** BLAME, CENSURE ⟨can't ∼ them for not coming⟩

3. In 1972 Dr. Thomas Starzl, the renowned Pittsburgh surgeon who **pioneered** liver transplants, stopped performing live-donor transplants of any kind.

   pioneer: _____

   ¹pi·o·neer \ˌpī-ə-'nir\ *n* [MF *pionier*, fr. OF *peonier* foot soldier, fr. *peon* foot soldier, fr. ML *pedon-, pedo* — more at PAWN] (1523) **1 :** a member of a military unit usu. of construction engineers **2 a :** a person or group that originates or helps open up a new line of thought or activity or a new method or technical development **b :** one of the first to settle in a territory **3 :** a plant or animal capable of establishing itself in a bare, barren, or open area and initiating an ecological cycle
   ²pioneer *vi* (1780) **:** to act as a pioneer ⟨∼ed in the development of airplanes⟩ ∼ *vt* **1 :** to open or prepare for others to follow; *also* : SETTLE **2 :** to originate or take part in the development of
   ³pioneer *adj* (1840) **1 :** ORIGINAL, EARLIEST **2 :** relating to or being a pioneer; *esp* : of, relating to, or characteristic of early settlers or their time

4. The drama of the Ayalas—making the baby, against such long odds, to save the older daughter—seemed to many to be a miracle. To others, it was **profoundly**, if sometimes obscurely, troubling.

profound: ─────────────────────────────

pro·found \prə-'faund, prō-\ *adj* [ME, fr. MF *profond* deep, fr. L *profundus*, fr. *pro-* before + *fundus* bottom — more at PRO-, BOTTOM] (14c) **1 a :** having intellectual depth and insight   **b :** difficult to fathom or understand   **2 a :** extending far below the surface   **b :** coming from, reaching to, or situated at a depth : DEEP-SEATED ⟨a ~ sigh⟩   **3 a** : characterized by intensity of feeling or quality   **b :** all encompassing : COMPLETE ⟨~ sleep⟩ — **pro·found·ly** \-'faun(d)-lē\ *adv* — **pro·found·ness** \-'faun(d)-nəs\ *n*

Pronunciation Guide

───

\ə\ **abut** \ʾ\ **kitten,** F **table** \ər\ **further** \a\ **ash** \ā\ **ace** \ä\ **mop, mar**
\aů\ **out** \ch\ **chin** \e\ **bet** \ē\ **easy** \g\ **go** \i\ **hit** \ī\ **ice** \j\ **job**
\ŋ\ **sing** \ō\ **go** \ȯ\ **law** \ȯi\ **boy** \th\ **thin** \<u>th</u>\ **the** \ü\ **loot** \ů\ **foot**
\y\ **yet** \zh\ **vision** \à, k̲, ⁿ, œ, œ̄, ᴇ, ᵫ, ʸ\

• E. Critical Thinking

Read each question carefully. Write your response in the space provided. Remember that there is no one correct answer. Your response depends on what **you** think.

1. What do you think is Dr. Rudolf Brutoco's opinion of the Ayalas' decision to have another child in the hopes of saving their daughter's life?

   _____

   _____

   _____

2. a. Why did Dr. Starzl stop performing live-donor transplants of any kind?

   _____

   _____

   b. Why do other doctors regard the number of donors who have died as "miraculously low"?

   _____

   _____

3. Why will there be a "higher and higher importance, and risk," for living relatives who may become donors?

   _____

   _____

   _____

• Another Perspective

Two Parents Offer Their Daughter the Breath of Life— to No Avail

Time

1   Did Cindy and Roger Plum of Coon Rapids, Minnesota, overstep the limits of parental sacrifice to try to
save their 9-year-old daughter Alyssa? Although their
efforts failed, both parents say they would do it
5 again—and again.

  Last New Year's Eve, Alyssa took to bed with symptoms that suggested bronchitis. Three months later,
she was rushed to a hospital emergency room with a
high fever. Doctors suspected a virus, but sent her
10 home. Two days later, Alyssa was at her doctor's office
with pneumonia. Within days, her skin turned blue
from lack of oxygen. By mid-April she was on a list for
a lung transplant.

  The Plums, who had read about transplant surgeries
15 using lobes of the lung from living donors, decided to

Reprinted with permission from *Time* magazine, "The Gift of Life," Lance Morrow, June 17, 1991.

volunteer. Alyssa successfully received a piece of
Roger's lung. Then her other lung failed. Less than four
weeks later, Cindy underwent the procedure. This time
Alyssa died of heart failure. Both parents have 18-inch
20 scars that run from their chest to their back. Cindy's
sleep is still interrupted by pain. Roger suffers from
muscle weakness. Even though the couple have a son,
Travis, six, who risked losing a parent, they never had
doubts about their actions. "If I didn't give Alyssa a
25 chance at life," says Cindy, "I didn't know if I could live
with myself."

• Questions for "Two Parents Offer Their Daughter the Breath of Life—to No Avail"

1. a. How many lung lobe transplants did Alyssa receive?

   _____

   b. Were they successful?

   _____

2. Why did six-year-old Travis risk losing a parent?

   _____

   _____

3. a. What adverse effects do Cindy and Roger Plum suffer from the transplants?

   _____

   _____

   b. Do the Plums have any regrets about the transplants?

   _____

• F. Follow-up Activities

1. Refer to the **Self-Evaluation of Reading Strategies** on the next page. Think about the strategies you used to help yourself understand "The Gift of Life." Check off the strategies you used. Evaluate your strategy use over the first nine chapters. Which strategies have you begun to use that you didn't use before? Which strategies do you use consistently? Which strategies have you added to the list? Which strategies are becoming automatic? To what extent have you applied these strategies to other reading you do?

Self-Evaluation of Reading Strategies

Strategies	Readings		
	"Matters of Life and Death"	"Sales of Kidneys"	"The Gift of Life"
I read the title and try to predict what the reading will be about.			
I use my knowledge of the world to help me understand the text.			
I read as though I *expect* the text to have meaning.			
I use illustrations to help me understand the text.			
I ask myself questions about the text.			
I use a variety of types of context clues.			
I take chances in order to identify meaning.			
I continue if I am not successful.			
I identify and underline main ideas.			
I connect details with main ideas.			
I summarize the reading in my own words.			
I skip unnecessary words.			
I look up words correctly in the dictionary.			
I connect the reading to other material I have read.			
I do not translate into my native language.			

2. Conduct an in-class survey using the questions in the following chart. Record the responses on the chart. (You may use your data later if you decide to do an out-of-class survey on the same questions.) Discuss the responses in class.

Questions	Yes	No
1. Is it morally acceptable for parents to conceive a child in order to obtain an organ or tissue to save the life of another one of their children?		
2. Is it morally acceptable to remove a kidney or other nonessential organ from a living person for use in another person's body?		
3. Would you donate a kidney for transplant to a close relative who needed it?		
4. Is it ethical to ask a child under the age of 18 to give up a kidney for a transplant to a relative?		
5. If you or a close relative had a fatal disease that could possibly be cured by a transplant, which of these would you be willing to do? a. Purchase the necessary organ or tissue b. Conceive a child to provide the necessary organ or tissue c. Take legal action to force a relative to donate		

• G. Topics for Discussion and Writing

1. In a recent magazine survey, 47% of American people said that they believe it is acceptable for parents to conceive a child in order to obtain an organ or tissue to save the life of another one of their children. However, 37% of American people believe that this would be unacceptable. What do you think? Write a letter to the magazine in support of or against this idea. Be sure to make your reasons clear.

2. In your country, what do you think is the general opinion on living-to-living organ donation (for example, a kidney or a lung lobe)? Is this practice legal? Write a paragraph about this type of organ donation in your country. When you are finished, compare it with your classmates' descriptions of organ donation in their countries. How are the policies similar in various countries? How are they different?

3. **Write in your journal.** What is your opinion about the Ayala case? Do you approve of their decision to have another child in order to save their older daughter? Explain your opinion.

Unit III Review

• H. Crossword Puzzle

• Crossword Puzzle Clues

Across

2. an electronic device that controls the heartbeat
4. a thin plastic tube
7. kidneys, heart, lungs, pancreas, liver
12. direct one's efforts or attention to
13. poor
14. reflex; involuntary
19. sacrifice oneself
20. the exercise of a profession
21. best
23. referring to a disagreement or argument
24. looking back at a past event
25. a subject of investigation

Down

1. deadly; terminal
3. necessary
5. a system of moral values
6. a person who gives something voluntarily
8. a dead body; a corpse
9. judge
10. make known
11. relatives
15. keep in an existing state
16. solution
17. minor; trivial
18. part of a longer reading
22. the center part of bone

UNIT IV
The Environment

SOUTHEAST ASIAN
RAIN FOREST

THE WORLD'S MAJOR
RAIN FORESTS

AMAZON
RAIN FOREST

AFRICAN
RAIN FOREST

Playing with Fire

• Prereading Preparation

1. The title "Playing with Fire" has a double meaning. In other words, it has two meanings: a literal meaning and a figurative meaning.

   a. What is the literal meaning of "Playing with Fire"?
   b. What is the figurative meaning of "Playing with Fire"?

2. What is a rain forest? Where are rain forests located?

3. The rain forests of the Amazon are being destroyed. The following questions will be discussed in this article. Work with a partner. Write down any answers that you may have to these questions. After you have finished the article, check and complete your answers.

Questions	Answers
1. Who or what is destroying the rain forests?	
2. How are the rain forests being destroyed?	
3. Why are the rain forests being destroyed?	
4. How can rain forests be important to people?	
5. How can rain forests be important to the environment?	

Playing with Fire

by Laura Lopen, Rio de Janeiro,
John Maier, Porto Velho, and
Dick Thompson, Washington

Time

1   The skies over western Brazil will soon be dark both
day and night. Dark from the smoke of thousands of fires,
as farmers and cattle ranchers engage in their annual rite
of destruction: clearing land for crops and livestock by
5   burning the rain forests of the Amazon. Unusually heavy
rains have slowed down the burning this year, but the dry
season could come at any time, and then the fires will
reach a peak. Last year the smoke grew so thick that Porto
Velho, the capital of the state of Rondonia, was forced to
10   close its airport for days at a time. An estimated 12,250
square miles of Brazilian rain forest—an area larger than
Belgium—was reduced to ashes. . . .
      After years of inattention, the whole world has awak-
ened at last to how much is at stake in the Amazon. It
15   has become the front line in the battle to rescue earth's
endangered environment from humanity's destructive
ways. "Save the rain forest," long a rallying cry for con-
servationists, is now being heard from politicians, pun-
dits and rock stars. The movement has sparked a
20   confrontation between rich industrial nations, which are
fresh converts to the environmental cause, and the
poorer nations of the Third World, which view outside
interference as an assault on their sovereignty. . . .
      The vast region of unbroken green that surrounds the
25   Amazon River and its tributaries has been under assault
by settlers and developers for 400 years. Time and
again, the forest has defied predictions that it was
doomed. But now the danger is more real and imminent
than ever before as loggers level trees, dams flood vast
30   tracts of land and gold miners poison rivers with mercury. In Peru the forests are being cleared to grow coca
for cocaine production. "It's dangerous to say the forest
will disappear by a particular year," says Philip Fearnside
of Brazil's National Institute for Research in the Amazon,
35   "but unless things change, the forest *will* disappear."
      That would be more than a South American disas-
ter. It would be an incalculable catastrophe for the entire planet. Moist tropical forests are distinguished by
their canopies of interlocking leaves and branches that
40   shelter creatures below from sun and wind, and by

their incredible variety of animal and plant life. If the
forests vanish, so will more than one million species—
a significant part of the earth's biological diversity and
genetic heritage. Moreover, the burning of the Amazon
45 could have dramatic effects on global weather patterns—for example, heightening the warming trend
that may result from the greenhouse effect. . . .

The river and forest system covers 2.7 million
square miles (almost 90% of the area of the contiguous
50 United States) and stretches into eight countries besides Brazil. . . . The jungle is so dense and teeming
that all the biologists on earth could not fully describe
its life forms. A 1982 U.S. National Academy of Sciences report estimated that a typical four-square-mile
55 patch of rain forest may contain 750 species of trees,
125 kinds of mammals, 400 types of birds, 100 of rep-
tiles and 60 of amphibians. Each type of tree may support more than 400 insect species. . . .

But the diversity of the Amazon is more than just
60 good material for TV specials. The rain forest is a virtually untapped storehouse of evolutionary achievement
that will prove increasingly valuable to mankind as it
yields its secrets. Agronomists see the forest as a cor-
nucopia of undiscovered food sources, and chemists
65 scour the flora and fauna for compounds with seem-
ingly magical properties. For instance, the piquia tree
produces a compound that appears to be toxic to leaf-
cutter ants, which cause millions of dollars of damage
each year to South American agriculture. Such chemi-
70 cals promise attractive alternatives to dangerous syn-
thetic pesticides. Other jungle chemicals have already
led to new treatments for hypertension and some forms
of cancer. The lessons encoded in the genes of the
Amazon's plants and animals may ultimately hold the
75 key to solving a wide range of human problems.

Scientists are concerned that the destruction of the
Amazon could lead to climatic chaos. Because of the
huge volume of clouds it generates, the Amazon system plays a major role in the way the sun's heat is dis-
80 tributed around the globe. Any disturbance of this
process could produce far-reaching, unpredictable effects. Moreover, the Amazon region stores at least 75
billion tons of carbon in its trees, which when burned
spew carbon dioxide into the atmosphere. Since the air
85 is already dangerously overburdened by carbon dioxide from the cars and factories of industrial nations,

the torching of the Amazon could magnify the greenhouse effect—the trapping of heat by atmospheric CO_2.
90 No one knows just what impact the buildup of CO_2 will
have, but some scientists fear that the globe will begin
to warm up, bringing on wrenching climatic changes.

The forest functions like a delicately balanced organism that recycles most of its nutrients and much of
95 its moisture.[1] Wisps of steam float from the top of the
endless palette of green as water evaporates off the
upper leaves, cooling the trees as they collect the intense sunlight. Air currents over the forest gather this
evaporation into clouds, which return the moisture to
100 the system in torrential rains. Dead animals and veg-
etation decompose quickly, and the resulting nutrients
move rapidly from the soil back to growing plants. The
forest is such an efficient recycler that virtually no de-
caying matter seeps into the region's rivers.

105 In the early 1970s Brazil built the Trans-Amazon
Highway, a system of roads that run west from the
coastal city of Recife toward the Peruvian border. The
idea was to prompt a land rush similar to the pioneering of the American West. To encourage settlers to
110 brave the jungle, the government offered transportation and other incentives, allowing them to claim land
that they had "improved" by cutting down the trees.

But for most of the roughly 8,000 families that heeded
the government's call between 1970 and 1974, the dream
115 turned into a bitter disappointment. The soil, unlike the
rich sod in the Western United States, was so poor that
crop yields began to deteriorate badly after three or four
years. Most settlers eventually gave up and left. . . .

If the rain forest disappears, the process will begin
120 at its edges. While the Amazon forest as a whole generates roughly half of its own moisture, the percentage is
much higher in these western states, far from the At-
lantic. This means that deforestation is likely to have a
more dramatic impact on the climate in the west than
125 it would in the east. The process of deforestation could
become self-perpetuating as heat, drying and wind
cause the trees to die on their own. . . .

Perhaps the best hope for the forests' survival is the
growing recognition that they are more valuable when
130 left standing than when cut. Charles Peters of the Institute of Economic Botany at the New York Botanical Gar-
den recently published the results of a three-year study

---

[1] Refer to the graphic on page 197 for an illustration of this recycling process.

that calculated the market value of rubber and exotic produce like the Aguaje palm fruit that can be har-
135 vested from the Amazonian jungle. The study, which appeared in the British journal *Nature*, asserts that over time selling these products could yield more than twice the income of either cattle ranching or lumbering.

But if the burning of the forests goes on much
140 longer, the damage may become irreversible. Long before the great rain forests are destroyed altogether, the impact of deforestation on climate could dramatically change the character of the area, lead to mass extinctions of plant and animal species, and leave Brazil's
145 poor to endure even greater misery than they do now. The people of the rest of the world, no less than the Brazilians, need the Amazon, as a functioning system, and in the end, this is more important than the issue of who owns the forest. The Amazon may run through
150 South America, but the responsibility for saving the rain forests belongs to everyone.

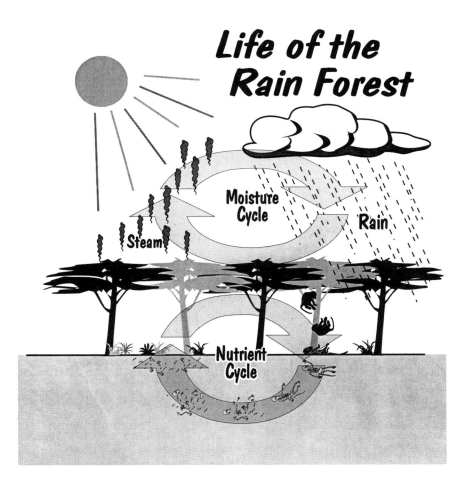

Life of the Rain Forest

• A. Reading Overview: Main Idea, Details, and Summary

Read the passage again. As you read, underline what you think are the most important ideas in the reading. Then, in one or two sentences, write the main idea of the reading. *Use your own words.*

Main idea:

_____

_____

_____

Details:

Use the outline below to organize the information in the reading. Refer back to the information you underlined in the passage as a guide. When you have finished, write a brief summary of the reading. *Use your own words.*

Playing with Fire

I. The Destruction of the Amazon Rain Forests

   A. by loggers, who cut down trees

   B.

   C.

   D.

   E.

II.

   A.

   B. It may change global weather patterns.

   C.

III. Overview of How Brazilian Rain Forests Became Endangered

   A.

   B.

   C. The poor soil failed in a few years.

IV. Advantages of Maintaining the Rain Forests

    A.

    B.

    C.

    D.

Summary:

_____

_____

_____

_____

• B. Statement Evaluation

Read the following statements. Then scan the article again quickly to find out if each sentence is **True (T), False (F),** or an **Inference (I).**

1. _____ According to this article, a large part of the Brazilian rain forest was burned last year.

2. _____ People have been destroying the Amazon rain forests for a long time.

3. _____ Industrialized nations can better afford to improve environmental conditions than can Third World nations.

4. _____ Few species of plants and animals live in the Amazon rain forest.

5. _____ The rain forests can be very important to mankind in ways that we are not yet aware of.

6. _____ Destruction of the Amazon can greatly affect the earth's weather patterns.

7. _____ The settlers of the Brazilian jungle in the early 1970s wanted to build a new life for themselves.

• C. Reading Analysis

Read each question carefully. Either circle the letter or number of the correct answer, or write your answer in the space provided.

1. Read lines 1–12.

   a. What is **"their annual rite of destruction"**?

      1. raising crops and livestock
      2. burning the Amazon rain forests
      3. the dark skies over western Brazil

   b. Why did the smoke grow so thick last year in Porto Velho?

      _____

2. In lines 12, 23, and elsewhere, there are ellipses (....) at the end of the paragraph. These dots indicate that

   a. the last sentence is incomplete
   b. text has been deleted from the article
   c. there are exactly three sentences missing

3. Read lines 13–17. What does **inattention** mean?

   a. not paying attention
   b. paying attention

4. Read lines 26–35.

   a. **Time and again** means

      1. the last time
      2. many times
      3. at one time

   b. **Imminent** means

      1. something will happen a long time from now
      2. something will happen soon

   c. Why is the danger **"more real and imminent than ever be-fore"**?

      _____

5. Read lines 41–47. **Moreover** means

   a. however
   b. although
   c. furthermore

6. Read lines 48–58. Why couldn't **all the biologists on earth fully describe its life forms?**

   a. because there are so many life forms
   b. because the life forms are hard to find
   c. because the life forms are far away

7. Read lines 76–92.

   a. What is **the greenhouse effect?**

   _____

   b. In lines 89 and 90, CO_2 is the chemical symbol for

   _____

8. Read lines 93–104. What does **recycle** mean?

   a. go around in a circle again
   b. extract and use again
   c. to fill up with moisture

9. Read lines 105–112. There are quotation marks (" ") around **improved** because the author

   a. wants to emphasize the improvement
   b. is stating a fact
   c. doesn't believe it really is improved

10. Read lines 118–127. **Deforestation** is

    a. the disappearance of the forest
    b. the climate of the forest
    c. the moisture of the forest

11. Read lines 135–138. What is *Nature*?

    _____

• D. Dictionary Skills

Read the entry for each word, and consider the context of the sentence from the passage. Write the entry number and the definition that is appropriate for the context on the line next to the word. Write the entry number too when appropriate. Be prepared to explain your choice.

1. The "save the rain forest" movement has sparked a confrontation between rich industrial nations, which are **fresh** converts to the environmental cause, and the poorer nations of the Third World, which view outside interference as an assault on their sovereignty.

   fresh: _____

   fresh \'fresh\ *adj* [ME, fr. OF *freis,* of Gmc origin; akin to OHG *frisc* fresh, OE *fersc* fresh] (13c) **1   a** : having its original qualities unimpaired: as (1) : full of or renewed in vigor : REFRESHED ⟨rose ∼ from a good night's sleep⟩ (2) : not stale, sour, or decayed ⟨∼ bread⟩ (3) : not faded ⟨the lessons remain ∼ in her memory⟩ (4) : not worn or rumpled ⟨a ∼ white shirt⟩ **b** : not altered by processing ⟨∼ vegetables⟩ **2   a** : not salt **b** (1) : free from taint : PURE ⟨∼ air⟩ (2) *of wind* : moderately strong **3   a** (1) : experienced, made, or received newly or anew ⟨form ∼ friendships⟩ (2) : ADDITIONAL, ANOTHER ⟨a ∼ start⟩ **b** : ORIGINAL, VIVID ⟨a ∼ portrayal⟩ **c** : lacking experience : RAW **d** : newly or just come or arrived ⟨∼ from school⟩ **e** : having the milk flow recently established ⟨a ∼ cow⟩ **4** [prob. by folk etymology fr. G *frech*] : disposed to take liberties : IMPUDENT   *syn* see NEW — **fresh·ly** *adv* — **fresh·ness** *n*

2. But now the danger is more real than ever before as loggers **level** trees and dams flood vast tracts of land.

   level: _____

   level *vb* **-eled** *or* **-elled; -el·ing** *or* **-el·ling** \'le-və-liŋ, 'lev-liŋ\ *vt* (15c) **1** : to make (a line or surface) horizontal : make flat or level ⟨∼ a field⟩ ⟨∼ off a house lot⟩ **2   a** : to bring to a horizontal aiming position **b** : AIM, DIRECT ⟨∼ed a charge of fraud⟩ **3** : to bring to a common level or plane : EQUALIZE ⟨love ∼s all ranks —W. S. Gilbert⟩ **4   a** : to lay level with or as if with the ground : RAZE **b** : to knock down ⟨∼ed him with one punch⟩ **5** : to make (as color) even or uniform **6** : to find the heights of different points in (a piece of land) esp. with a surveyor's level ∼ *vi* **1** : to attain or come to a level ⟨the plane ∼ed off at 10,000 feet⟩ **2** : to aim a gun or other weapon horizontally **3** : to bring persons or things to a level **4** : to deal frankly and openly

Pronunciation Guide

\ə\ **abut** \ʼ\ **kitten,** F **table** \ər\ **further** \a\ **ash** \ā\ **ace** \ä\ **mop, mar**
\au̇\ **out** \ch\ **chin** \e\ **bet** \ē\ **easy** \g\ **go** \i\ **hit** \ī\ **ice** \j\ **job**
\ŋ\ **sing** \ō\ **go** \ȯ\ **law** \ȯi\ **boy** \th\ **thin** \t̲h̲\ **the** \ü\ **loot** \u̇\ **foot**
\y\ **yet** \zh\ **vision** \a̱, k̲, ⁿ, œ, œ̄, ue, ūe, ʸ\

3. Brazil built the Trans-Amazon Highway in the early 1970s. The idea was to **prompt** a land rush similar to the pioneering of the American West.

prompt: _____

¹**prompt** \'präm(p)t\ *vt* [ME, fr. ML *promptare*, fr. L *promptus* prompt] (14c) **1 :** to move to action : INCITE **2 :** to assist (one acting or reciting) by suggesting or saying the next words of something forgotten or imperfectly learned : CUE **3 :** to serve as the inciting cause of — **prompt·er** *n*
²**prompt** *adj* (1784) : of or relating to prompting actors
³**prompt** *adj* [ME, fr. MF or L; MF, fr. L *promptus* ready, prompt, fr. pp. of *promere* to bring forth, fr. *pro-* forth + *emere* to take — more at REDEEM] (15c) **1 :** being ready and quick to act as occasion demands **2 :** performed readily or immediately ⟨~ assistance⟩ *syn* see QUICK — **prompt·ly** \'präm(p)t-lē, 'präm-plē\ *adv* — **prompt·ness** \'präm(p)t-nəs, 'prämp-nəs\ *n*
⁴**prompt** *n, pl* **prompts** \'präm(p)ts, 'prämps\ (1597) **1** [¹*prompt*] : something that prompts : REMINDER **2** [³*prompt*] : a limit of time given for payment of an account for goods purchased; *also* : the contract by which this time is fixed

4. Charles Peters recently published the results of a three-year **study** that calculated the market value of rubber.

study: _____

study \'stə-dē\ *n, pl* **stud·ies** [ME *studie*, fr. OF *estudie*, fr. L *studium*, fr. *studēre* to devote oneself, study; prob. akin to L *tundere* to beat — more at CONTUSION] (14c) **1 :** a state of contemplation : REVERIE **2 a** : application of the mental faculties to the acquisition of knowledge ⟨years of ~⟩ **b** : such application in a particular field or to a specific subject ⟨the ~ of Latin⟩ **c** : careful or extended consideration ⟨the proposal is under ~⟩ **d** (1) : a careful examination or analysis of a phenomenon, development, or question (2) : the published report of such a study **3 :** a building or room devoted to study or literary pursuits **4 :** PURPOSE, INTENT **5 a** : a branch or department of learning : SUBJECT **b** : the activity or work of a student ⟨returning to her *studies* after vacation⟩ **c** : an object of study or deliberation ⟨every gesture a careful ~ —Marcia Davenport⟩ **d** : something attracting close attention or examination **6 :** a person who learns or memorizes something (as a part in a play) — usu. used with a qualifying adjective ⟨he's a fast ~⟩ **7 :** a literary or artistic production intended as a preliminary outline, an experimental interpretation, or an exploratory analysis of specific features or characteristics **8 :** a musical composition for the practice of a point of technique

• E. Critical Thinking

Read each question carefully. Write your response in the space provided. Remember that there is no one correct answer. Your response depends on what **you** think.

1. The authors state that "the movement [to save the rain forests] has sparked a confrontation between rich industrial nations, which are fresh converts to the environmental cause, and the poorer nations of the Third World." Where are Third World countries located? Why do you think rich industrial nations are apparently more interested in environmental issues than are poorer Third World countries?

   _____

   _____

2. The authors are clearly in favor of preserving the Amazon rain forest. Are all their arguments persuasive? What are their strongest arguments? What are their weakest arguments?

   _____

   _____

   _____

   _____

3. The last sentence in the article states that "the responsibility for saving the rain forest belongs to everyone." What do you think the Brazilian government and the Brazilian people's attitude is about this statement? Explain your reasons.

   _____

   _____

   _____

4. According to the authors, the rain forest system extends into eight countries besides Brazil. Why do you think the authors focused on Brazil and didn't give equal mention to the other eight countries?

   _____

   _____

   _____

• Another Perspective

Taking Two Steps Back

by Mac Margolis
Newsweek

1   Imagine a great plume of smoke, big enough to
stretch from the Rockies to Rhode Island, blotting out
the sun and the moon. The Amazon, crown jewel of the
world's rain forests, is burning—again. From June to
5 November last year, tens of thousands of fires blazed
over the two million square miles of the Brazilian Amazon. Winds swept the pall of smoke across distant bor-
ders, shrouding the land and choking cities for
hundreds of miles. Hospitals reported a surge in pa-
10 tients with bronchial problems. Smoke-blinded motorists smashed into each other on the highways. "It was
like Los Angeles come to the Amazon," said Elaine
Prins, a University of Wisconsin scientist studying the
effect of the burning on the world's climate.
15   This was not the worst season of *queimadas*
(burnings) ever. But the renewed binge was a cruel reminder to defenders of the Amazon that their battle was
not yet won. The fires soured a recent memorial service

for Francisco (Chico) Alves Mendes, the union leader and
20 environmentalist whose protests against land-clearing
ranchers—and 1988 murder—turned the rape of rain forests into a worldwide scandal. And the burning mocked
the message of the 1992 Earth Summit in Rio de Janeiro,
where Brazil answered critics by backing sweeping trea-
25 ties to protect the environment. That year, all the attention seemed to be paying off. The government announced
that the rate at which the rain forest was disappearing
had been cut to half what it was in the 1980s, when an
area the size of Massachusetts was lost every year.
30   The *queimadas* tradition, as old as agriculture, has
proved almost impossible to uproot. And although the
government took credit for curbing the practice, a sour
economy may have had more to do with the progress
in the early 1990s. "Ranchers simply did not have the
35 money" to expand, argues Philip Fearnside of the Brazilian Institute of Amazon Studies. Now Brazil's
economy is rebounding and many farmers are beginning to expand again. And at the same time, drought
made it easier to set fires and keep them going. Exactly
40 how badly the fight against illegal land burning has
gone this season is hard to say. Since 1992 the government has failed to come up with funds for an annual
survey of the Amazon basin. "We were promised the
funds, but they never came," says Volcker Kirchhoff,
45 director of the Brazilian Space Institute. Still, institute
researchers used satellite photos to document more
than 150,000 fires throughout Brazil this season and
no fewer than 95,000 in Amazonia.
    Defenders of the Amazon have reawakened with a
50 start. INFERNO ON THE GREEN FRONTIER, said a recent
cover of *Veja*, the nation's leading news weekly. Ecol-
ogy activists and defenders of Brazil's Indians have be-
sieged president Fernando Henrique Cardoso with
petitions. Surly crowds of greens confronted the head
55 of Brazil's environmental-protection agency, Raul
Jungmann, on a recent trip to Washington.
    The government calls it hype.[1] "The headlines are
way out of proportion," Jungmann says. Besides making other arguments, government officials suggest that
60 many of the latest fires were set to restore overgrown

---

[1] Hype is a term used, usually negatively, to describe exaggerated claims or
    publicity, often through the media.

pastures and fields, not to clear virgin forest. Still,
only now has Brasilia come up with $2.4 million for a
detailed survey of the last three years' damage to the
rain forest. It's already clear that protecting the Ama-
65 zon basin may be as difficult as grabbing smoke.

• Questions for "Taking Two Steps Back"

1. What were some direct results of the most recent rain forest
   burnings?

   _____

   _____

   _____

2. Who was Francisco Alves Mendes? Why do you think he might
   have been murdered?

   _____

   _____

3. a. What may be the reason that the number of burnings de-
      creased in Brazil in the early 1990s?

      _____

      _____

   b. What may be one reason why the number of burnings has re-
      cently started to increase?

      _____

      _____

4. a. How does the government explain the latest fires?

      _____

      _____

   b. Do you think the author agrees or disagrees with the Brazil-
      ian government's explanation? Why?

      _____

      _____

• F. Follow-up Activities

1. Refer to the **Self-Evaluation of Reading Strategies** on pages 250–251. Think about the strategies you used to help yourself understand "Playing with Fire." Check off the strategies you used. Think about the strategies you didn't use, and try to apply them to help yourself understand the readings that follow.

2. Look at the following chart carefully, then answer the questions that follow.

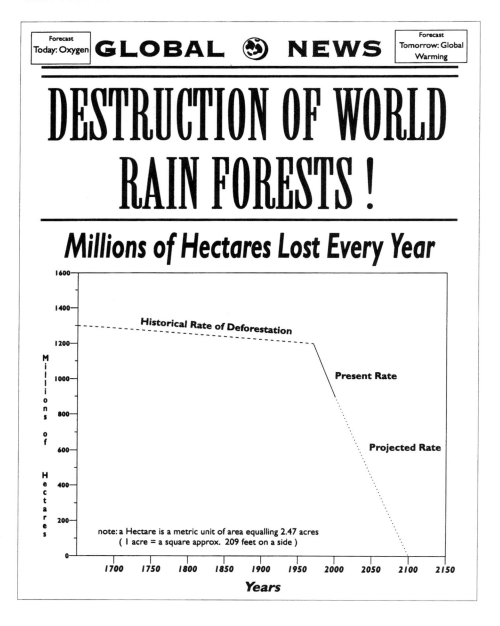

a. What does this chart illustrate?

_____

b. How many hectares of rain forest existed in the world in 1950?

_____

c. According to this chart, how many hectares of rain forest will exist in the world in the year 2100?

_____

d. The chart shows the projected rate of destruction of the rain forests between the years 2000 and 2100.

　1. What does **projected rate** mean?

_____

　2. What is this rate based on?

_____

　3. How can this rate be changed?

_____

3. Form a panel of experts. Research the global effects of deforestation in the Amazon. Present and discuss solutions to the conflict between the development of Brazil and the preservation of the rain forest. Propose both short-term and long-range plans to satisfy both the immediate needs of Brazil and its citizens as well as the goals of environmentalists.

4. a. Prepare an interview with the President of Brazil. You must be very diplomatic because the President did not really want to be interviewed, but feels he must improve his public image and that of his country. You want to present Brazil in a positive light. Ask questions that will elicit sympathy for the situation in Brazil and show how the government is trying to improve conditions now and over the next few decades. Give the President the opportunity to respond to negative comments about Brazilian government policy and the deforestation of the Amazon jungle.

　b. Have one or two students volunteer to play the role of the President of Brazil. Have a panel of three or four students act as interviewers. With the other classmates as an audience, conduct an interview. When you are finished, review the interviewers' questions and the President's replies.

• G. Topics for Discussion and Writing

1. There are many different ways in which people are destroying our environment. There are also many different ways in which people are trying to preserve our environment. Give some examples of both actions.

2. What are some ways that this issue can be resolved with a compromise between environmentalists and people who are clearing the rain forests?

3. In the United States, many people are concerned about recycling waste. Do you think this is important? Why or why not? Is your country also concerned with recycling? Why or why not?

4. **Write in your journal.** Do you think it is important to save rain forests? Why or why not?

Wilder Places for Wild Things

• Prereading Preparation

1. Work with one or two partners. What do you know about traditional zoos? What do you know about modern zoos? Complete the following chart.

Traditional Zoos	Modern Zoos

2. Why do you think zoos have changed in these ways?

3. What do you like the most about traditional zoos? Modern zoos? What do you like the least? Why?

4. Read the title of this article. What aspect of zoos do you think the reading will focus on?

Wilder Places for Wild Things

by Sharon Begley with Karen Springen in Chicago,
Jeanne Gordon in Los Angeles, Daniel Glick in Washington,
and Howard Manley in Atlanta
Newsweek

1   The beavers at the Minnesota Zoo seem engaged in
an unending task. Each week they fell scores of inch-
thick young trees for their winter food supply. Each
week zoo workers surreptitiously replace the downed
5   trees, anchoring new ones in the iron holders so the
animals can keep on cutting. Letting the beavers do
what comes naturally has paid off: Minnesota is one of
the few zoos to get them to reproduce in captivity. The
chimps at the St. Louis Zoo also work for a living: they
10   poke stiff pieces of hay into an anthill to scoop out the
baby food and honey that curators hide inside. Instead
of idly awaiting banana handouts, the chimps get to
manipulate tools, just as they do in the wild. Last year,
when 13 gorillas moved into Zoo Atlanta's new $4.5
15   million rain forest, they mated and formed families—a
rarity among captives. "Zoos have changed from being
mere menageries to being celebrations of life," says
John Gwynne of the Bronx Zoo. "As the wild places get
smaller, the role of zoos gets larger, which means in-
20   tensifying the naturalness of the experience for both
visitors and animals."
     Naturalistic zoos are hardly new: animals liberated
from concrete cages have been romping on Bronx sa-
vannas since 1941. But as species become extinct at a
25   rate unparalleled since the Cretaceous era and 100
acres of tropical forests vanish every minute, zoos are
striving to make their settings match their new role as
keepers of the biological flame. Since 1980 the nation's
143 accredited zoos and aquariums have spent more
30   than $1 billion on renovation and construction, much
of it going to create habitats that immerse both animals and visitors in the sights, sounds, feel and smell
of the wild. Today's best exhibits reproduce not just
the look but also the function of a natural habitat: they
35   encourage the residents to mate, to raise young and to
develop the survival skills they would need on the sa-
vannas of Africa or the slopes of the Andes. . . .

Lately curators have been making exhibits not only look real but sound real. At the Bronx Zoo's lush Jungle
40 World the shrieks of gibbons, the cacophony of crickets and the trills of hornbills emanate from 65 speakers. The zoo's resident audio expert, Tom Veltre, spent a month in Thailand stringing microphones and a mile of cables up and down mountains to capture the
45 sounds of the jungle. Even though the animals figure out that the hoots and howls are coming from black boxes, and not from furry or feathered neighbors, the call of the wild can shape their behavior. At Healesville Sanctuary, outside Melbourne, Australia, nighttime
50 sounds cue nocturnal platypuses when to sleep, says bio-acoustician Leslie Gilbert; realistic noises also snap gorillas out of stress-induced lethargy.

"Natural" is now going beyond sight and sound to include everything from weather to activity patterns. Every
55 day 11 rainstorms hit Tropic World at the Brookfield Zoo outside Chicago, prompting the monkeys to drop from their vines and scamper for cover amid cliffs, 50-foot-high gunite trees and 6,000 tropical plants. Regardless of the climate, the monkeys exhibit an array of behav-
60 iors never displayed in cages, such as rustling bushes to define their territories. At the San Diego Zoo's Sun Bear Forest, lion-tailed macaques are surrounded by jungle vines and cascading waterfalls. As soon as these highly endangered monkeys moved in last month, they fanned
65 out and began foraging for fruit and other dainties left by the curators. They even respond to the dominant male's alarm call by clustering around him—something keepers had never seen. At Seattle's Woodland Park Zoo, elephants in the exhibit that opened last month roll and
70 stack logs just as they do in a Thai logging camp. The task relieves the pachyderms' boredom.

Curators of rare species are focusing on how to induce one particular natural behavior—reproduction. At New York's Central Park Zoo, which reopened last year
75 after a multimillion-dollar overhaul, the lights in the penguin house mimic seasonal changes in the austral day and night, which serve as a crucial cue for the birds' breeding cycle. At the San Diego Wild Animal Park, people are confined to cages (an electric mono-
80 rail) and 2,600 animals roam free on 700 acres of veld and savanna. A white rhino that had never mated dur-

ing 10 years at the San Diego Zoo has sired 55 offspring since moving into a 110-acre area at the park 17
years ago. "The difference is that he has room to mark
85 out his territory and a harem [of 20] from which to
choose," says spokesman Tom Hanscom. Getting fla-
mingos to breed was simply a matter of providing
more neighbors. For reasons curators can't explain, the
leggy pink birds never bred when they lived in two
90 flocks of 50. But when merged into a group of 100 they
began to build little mud mounds in the lake shallows
on which to lay their eggs.

Once fiercely competitive, most American zoos now
participate in species-survival programs, intricate dat-
95 ing games for animals living far apart. Coordinated by
the American Association of Zoological Parks and
Aquariums, the SSP's rely on studbooks that keep track
of zoo animals' age and ancestry, helping curators determine how to pair up males and females from mem-
100 ber zoos to maintain the species' health and avoid
inbreeding. Animals move back and forth between
zoos to ensure the best genetic mix. Right now Indian
rhinos from the Oklahoma City and National zoos are
cozying up to the Bronx Zoo's female.
105 Without such programs, many species would be extinct. "Zoos are becoming the last hope for a number of
endangered species," says Ronald Tilson of the Minnesota Zoo. Indeed, there are more Siberian tigers in
America's zoos than on Russia's northern tundra. For
110 all their breeding successes, though, zoos will become
little more than Noah's arks if nature continues to give
way to pavement. That's why the new naturalistic settings are designed with people in mind, too. "Part of a
zoo's reason for being is to inform the public of the
115 marvelous things that occur on this planet," says War-
ren Thomas, director of the Los Angeles Zoo. "You do
that by re-creating the environment that shaped these
animals." In zoo parlance, it's called habitat immersion: getting visitors curious and excited about wild
120 places and teaching them that habitat loss is the single
greatest threat to wild animals today.

In the rare cases when animals bred in captivity do
have an ancestral home to return to, zoos are trying to
oblige them. "The closer you come to mimicking nature
125 in captivity, the easier that is," says primate curator

Ann Baker of Brookfield. Already the Bronx Zoo has returned condors to the Andes. Scientists at the National
Zoo in Washington taught a group of golden lion tamarins survival skills, such as how to forage and to heed
130 warning calls, and have released 67 into a reserve near
Rio de Janeiro since 1984. Although 35 died, others not
only survived but mated; so far the freed animals have
produced 13 surviving offspring. The San Diego Park
has returned 49 oryxes—rare antelopes—to Oman, Jor-
135 dan and Israel, where the graceful creatures have bred
successfully. Black-footed ferrets, which a few years
ago had dwindled to only 17 in the wild, have proliferated to 125 in captivity, and scientists plan to release
the animals into prairie-dog territories in the Great
140 Plains in a few years.

     With every animal that moves onto the endangered
species list, or drops off it by extinction, zoos assume
greater importance. About 120 million people will visit
U.S. zoos this year, giving curators 120 million chances
145 to spread the conservation gospel. By showing how
animals are shaped and supported by their environment, "zoos are trying to protect wild places as well as
wild things," says Zoo Atlanta director Terry Maple. For
as the wild places go, so go the wild animals.

• A. Reading Overview: Main Idea, Details, and Summary

Read the passage again. As you read, underline what you think are the most important ideas in the reading. Then, in one or two sentences, write the main idea of the reading. *Use your own words.*

Main idea:

_____

_____

_____

Details:

Use the outline below to organize the information in the reading. Refer back to the information you underlined in the passage as a guide. When you have finished, write a brief summary of the reading. *Use your own words.*

Wilder Places for Wild Things

   I. Examples of Animal Behavior in Naturalistic Settings

      A.

      B.

      C.

  II. Zoos Re-create Animals' Natural Environment

     What zoos do:

     Examples:

     Results:

III.

      A. Purpose of the SSPs

         1.

         2.

         3.

B.

  1.

  2. The release of golden lion tamarins into a reserve in Brazil.

  3.

Summary:

_____

_____

_____

_____

• B. Statement Evaluation

Read the following statements. Then scan the article again quickly to find out if each sentence is **True (T), False (F),** or an **Opinion (O).**

1. _____ Beavers reproduce in most zoos.

2. _____ At the Minnesota Zoo, animals are able to get their own food instead of being fed.

3. _____ Naturalistic zoos are better than traditional zoos.

4. _____ Modern zoos do not encourage animals to learn how to survive in the wild.

5. _____ Zoo curators are arranging for animals from different zoos to reproduce together.

6. _____ Naturalistic zoos give people important information about an animal's natural environment.

7. _____ Animals are happier in naturalistic zoos than they are in traditional zoos.

• C. Reading Analysis

Read each question carefully. Either circle the letter or number of the correct answer, or write your answer in the space provided.

1. Read lines 8–13.

   a. What do the chimps at this zoo **work for?**

   _____

   b. What follows the colon (:)?

      1. an explanation
      2. an example
      3. a new idea

2. Read lines 13–16. What is **a rarity among captives?**

   _____

3. Read lines 16–21. **"The role of zoos gets larger"** means

   a. zoos are getting bigger
   b. zoos are becoming more important
   c. wild places are getting smaller

4. Read lines 38–52. Where do the realistic sounds in the zoos come from?

   a. the jungle
   b. the animals
   c. the speakers

5. Read lines 53–66.

   a. Why is the word **natural** in quotation marks (" ")?

   _____

   b. What does **regardless of** mean?

      1. in spite of
      2. instead of
      3. in addition to

   c. What does **these highly endangered monkeys** refer to?

   _____

6. Read lines 68–71.

   a. What word is a synonym for **pachyderms?**

   _____

   b. What does **just as** mean?

      1. only
      2. in the same way
      3. because of

7. Read lines 93–101. What is an **SSP**?

   _____

8. Read lines 122–127. **"Zoos are trying to oblige them"** means that zoos

   a. want to return animals to their natural environment
   b. want to keep the animals in captivity
   c. are trying to get the animals to reproduce

9. Read lines 133–140. What are **dwindled** and **proliferated**?

   a. numbers
   b. synonyms
   c. antonyms

10. Read lines 141–149.

   a. Animals that **drop off it by extinction**

      1. all die
      2. survive
      3. increase

   b. Read lines 148 and 149. This sentence means that when the animals' natural environment disappears,

      1. the animals will reproduce
      2. the animals will disappear, too
      3. the animals will prefer to live in zoos

• D. Dictionary Skills

Read the entry for each word, and consider the context of the sentence from the passage. Write the definition that is appropriate for the context on the line next to the word. Write the entry number too when appropriate. Be prepared to explain your choice.

1. Seasonal changes in the austral day and night serve as a crucial **cue** for the penguins' breeding cycle.

cue: _____

¹cue \'kyü\ *n* [ME *cu* half a farthing (spelled form of *q*, abbr. for L *quadrans* quarter of an as)] (ca. 1755) : the letter *q*
²cue *n* [prob. fr. *qu*, abbr. (used as a direction in actors' copies of plays) of L *quando* when] (1553) **1 a** : a signal (as a word, phrase, or bit of stage business) to a performer to begin a specific speech or action   **b** : something serving a comparable purpose : HINT **2** : a feature indicating the nature of something perceived   **3** *archaic* : the part one has to perform in or as if in a play   **4** *archaic* : MOOD, HUMOR
³cue *vt* **cued; cu·ing** *or* **cue·ing** (1922) **1** : to give a cue to : PROMPT   **2** : to insert into a continuous performance ⟨~ in sound effects⟩
⁴cue *n* [F *queue*, lit., tail, fr. L *cauda*] (ca. 1749) **1 a** : a leather-tipped tapering rod for striking the cue ball (as in billiards and pool)   **b** : a long-handled instrument with a concave head for shoving disks in shuffleboard   **2** : QUEUE 2
⁵cue *vb* **cued; cu·ing** *or* **cue·ing** *vt* (ca. 1784) **1** : QUEUE **2** : to strike with a cue ~ *vi* **1** : QUEUE **2** : to use a cue

2. Since 1980 the nation's 143 accredited zoos and aquariums have spent more than $1 billion on renovation and construction, much of it going to create habitats that **immerse** both animals and visitors in the sights, sounds, feel and smell of the wild.

   Part of a zoo's reason for being is to inform the public. You do that by re-creating the environment that shaped these animals. This is called habitat **immersion**: getting visitors curious and excited about wild places.

immerse: _____

im·merse \i-'mərs\ *vt* **im·mersed; im·mers·ing** [ME, fr. L *immersus*, pp. of *immergere*, fr. in- + *mergere* to merge] (15c) **1** : to plunge into something that surrounds or covers; *esp* : to plunge or dip into a fluid   **2** : ENGROSS, ABSORB ⟨completely *immersed* in his work⟩   **3** : to baptize by immersion

Pronunciation Guide

\ə\ abut \ʼ\ kitten, F table \ər\ further \a\ ash \ā\ ace \ä\ mop, mar
\au̇\ out \ch\ chin \e\ bet \ē\ easy \g\ go \i\ hit \ī\ ice \j\ job
\ŋ\ sing \ō\ go \ȯ\ law \ȯi\ boy \th\ thin \t̲h̲\ the \ü\ loot \u̇\ foot
\y\ yet \zh\ vision \à, k̲, ⁿ, œ, œ̄, ᵫ, ᵫ̄, ʸ\

3. The lights in the penguin house **mimic** seasonal changes in the austral day and night.

    The closer you can **mimic** nature in captivity, the easier it is to return animals to the wild.

mimic: _____

¹mim·ic \'mi-mik\ *n* (1590)   **1** : MIME 2   **2** : one that mimics
²mimic *adj* [L *mimicus,* fr. Gk *mimikos,* fr. *mimos* mime] (1598)   **1   a** : IMITATIVE   **b** : IMITATION, MOCK ⟨a ∼ battle⟩   **2** : of or relating to mime or mimicry
³mimic *vt* **mim·icked** \-mikt\; **mim·ick·ing** (1687)   **1** : to imitate closely : APE   **2** : to ridicule by imitation   **3** : SIMULATE   **4** : to resemble by biological mimicry   ***syn*** see COPY

4. When animals bred in captivity have a home to return to, zoos are trying to **oblige** them. Already the Bronx Zoo has returned condors to the Andes.

oblige: _____

oblige \ə-'blīj\ *vb* **obliged; oblig·ing** [ME, fr. OF *obliger,* fr. L *obligare,* lit., to bind to, fr. *ob-* toward + *ligare* to bind — more at LIGATURE] *vt* (14c)   **1** : to constrain by physical, moral, or legal force or by the exigencies of circumstance ⟨*obliged* to find a job⟩   **2   a** : to put in one's debt by a favor or service ⟨we are much *obliged* for your help⟩   **b** : to do a favor for ⟨always ready to ∼ a friend⟩   ∼ *vi* : to do something as or as if a favor   ***syn*** see FORCE — **oblig·er** *n*

• E. Critical Thinking

Read each question carefully. Write your response in the space provided. Remember that there is no one correct answer. Your response depends on what **you** think.

1. Why do you think zoos have taken on the responsibility of preserving endangered species?

   _____

   _____

   _____

2. The authors state that most American zoos were **"once fiercely competitive."** Why do you think zoos were competitive? Why do you think they are not competitive anymore?

   _____

   _____

   _____

3. Why are there more Siberian tigers in America's zoos than there are in Russia's northern tundra?

   _____

   _____

   _____

4. Why do zoos assume greater importance as more animals move onto the endangered species list?

   _____

   _____

• Another Perspective

Predators on the Prowl

by Marc Peyser with Daniel Glick
Newsweek

1   For Iris Kenna, Cuyamaga Rancho State Park near
San Diego was like a second home. By day, she strolled
its fields in search of exotic birds. At night, the 56-
year-old high-school counselor sometimes slept under
5   the stars. But one morning exactly a year ago, Kenna
encountered something unfamiliar, and it saw her first.
Without warning, a 140-pound male mountain lion
pounced on her from behind. The struggle was brief.
The animal dragged the dying 5-foot-4 Kenna into
10   dense brush to hide her from competing predators.
Rangers found her only after two hikers spotted a pair
of glasses, a backpack and a human tooth by the path
she had been on. The rangers followed a trail of her
clothes for 30 yards until they came to Kenna's body.
15   The back of her scalp was ripped off; the rest of her
was riddled with bites. No one had heard a scream, or
even a roar.

   Kenna is the most vivid symbol of an angry, shifting
debate over how people and predators can coexist. In
20   the high-growth Western states, many residents love living near the wild, and they are inclined to preserve it no
matter what the risks. But violent deaths like Kenna's—
and a string of other mountain-lion attacks—are making

a powerful case for fighting back. Californians will vote
in March on opening the way to mountain-lion hunting,
25 which has been prohibited there for more than 20 years.[1]
But Oregon, Arizona and Colorado recently changed
their hunting laws to ensure that predatory animals—including bears, wolves and coyotes—would be protected.
"It's overwhelmingly popular to have these animals in
30 our ecosystems," says Tom Dougherty of the National
Wildlife Federation. "But if they're in your backyard,
some people aren't loving it."

The most acute mountain-lion problem is in California. That's partly because the state's human population
35 has doubled every 25 years this century. As more
people built more houses, they usurped territory once
largely inhabited by wild animals. But the mountain lion
(alternately called cougar, puma and panther) has also
been questionably served by environmentalists. In
40 1972, preservation-minded Californians banned hunting
the majestic animals (except when they pose an imminent danger to people or livestock). The cougar population ballooned, from an estimated 2,400 lions to 6,000
today. Without hunters to thin the ranks, increased
45 competition for food has sent hungry mountain lions to
suburban backyards, shopping centers and elementary
schools in search of nourishment—a deer or, lacking
that, a dog. Even children have been mauled. "People are
afraid to go on a picnic without taking a firearm," says
50 state Senator Timi Leslie, a prominent anti-cougar advocate. In the wake of Kenna's death, Gov. Pete Wilson au-
thorized the March ballot initiative—one that could lead
to controlling the cougar population.

But in other places, sentiment favors animals at least
55 as much as people. A survey of Coloradans living near the
Rockies found that 80 percent believe that development
in mountain-lion territory should be restricted. What's
more, when wildlife authorities killed the cougar that
killed a woman named Barbara Schoener in California in
60 1994, donors raised $21,000 to care for the cougar's
cub—but only $9,000 for Schoener's two children.

---

[1] Postscript:In March, Californians once again voted against legalization of
mountain-lion hunting.

• Questions for "Predators on the Prowl"

1. How did Iris Kenna die?

   _____

   _____

2. a. What proposed law must Californians decide upon?

   _____

   _____

   b. What is the purpose of this proposed law?

   _____

   _____

   c. Why are some people against this proposed law?

   _____

   _____

3. Why has the mountain-lion problem in California increased over the years?

   _____

   _____

   _____

4. How do most people in Colorado feel about the mountain lions? What example do the authors give to support their belief?

   _____

   _____

5. What do you think is the authors' opinion of the mountain-lion situation in the western United States? Why do you think so?

   _____

   _____

   _____

• F. Follow-up Activities

1. Refer to the **Self-Evaluation of Reading Strategies** on pages 250–251. Think about the strategies you used to help yourself understand "Wilder Places for Wild Things." Check off the strategies you used. Think about the strategies you didn't use, and try to apply them to help yourself understand the readings that follow.

2. Work in small groups. You are journalists for a local television station in San Diego. You have been assigned to cover the use of state and municipal (i.e., local) funds that have recently been allocated to the San Diego Zoo. Prepare an interview with the curator of the San Diego Zoo. In your interview, include questions about the justification of this amount of money for the zoo's long-range goals. For example, what will the zoo do with the money? Why should the zoo have gotten such funding? Why should the residents of San Diego and California support such a project? Remember to add some questions of your own. When you have finished, exchange your questions with another group of classmates' questions. Try to answer their questions as they try to answer yours. When you are finished, compare your responses. Have the curators" answered the "interviewers'" questions convincingly?

3. Work in small groups. What do you think of the problem described in "Predators on the Prowl"? How do you think the problem can be solved? Write a list of your group's suggestions. Then compare your list with your classmates'. Decide which two or three suggestions are the best solutions.

• G. Topics for Discussion and Writing

1. According to the article, many endangered species raised in zoos were released into the wild. Many of these animals died. Do you think it is good practice for zoos to release these endangered animals and risk their death in the wild? Discuss your opinion with your classmates.

2. Compare the zoos in this country with zoos in your country and in other countries. How are they similar? How are they different?

3. Many zoo curators and other specialists are trying to save species of animals from extinction. Do you think it is important to try to preserve these animals? Explain your point of view.

4. **Write in your journal.** Refer to "Predators on the Prowl." Think about the amount of money that was raised for the victim's two children compared to the money raised for the cougar's cub. What is your opinion about this?

C·H·A·P·T·E·R 12

A Nuclear Graveyard

• Prereading Preparation

One of the greatest environmental concerns facing the world today is the disposal of nuclear waste. Much of this waste comes from nuclear power plants. (Refer to the illustration on page 252. You may want to do the exercise related to the illustration before you read the article.) In the United States, for example, the government is looking for a safe place to bury its nuclear waste. Currently the federal government is focusing on one particular site: the Yucca Mountains in the state of Nevada. Read the following paragraph, which is the first part of the article. Then answer the questions.

A Nuclear Graveyard

1   The apocalyptic scenario begins with an earthquake
near Yucca Mountain, a barren ridge 90 miles north-
west of Las Vegas that is the burial site for the nation's
most lethal nuclear waste. The tremor is minor; but
5   fresh movement in the earth's crust causes ground water to well up suddenly, flooding the repository. Soon,
a lethal brew of nuclear poisons seeps into the water
that flows underground to nearby Death Valley. Insects, birds and animals drink at the valley's contami-
10 nated springs, and slowly the radioactivity spreads
into the biosphere. "It would be a terrible disaster,"
says Charles Archambeau, a geophysicist at the University of Colorado.

   1. What does this paragraph describe?

      a. It describes what may happen if there is an earthquake at the place where the nuclear waste is buried.

      b. It describes what happens during all earthquakes.

2. Work with a partner to complete the following flowchart. According to the above paragraph, what is the chain of events that would lead to **"radioactivity spreading into the biosphere"**?

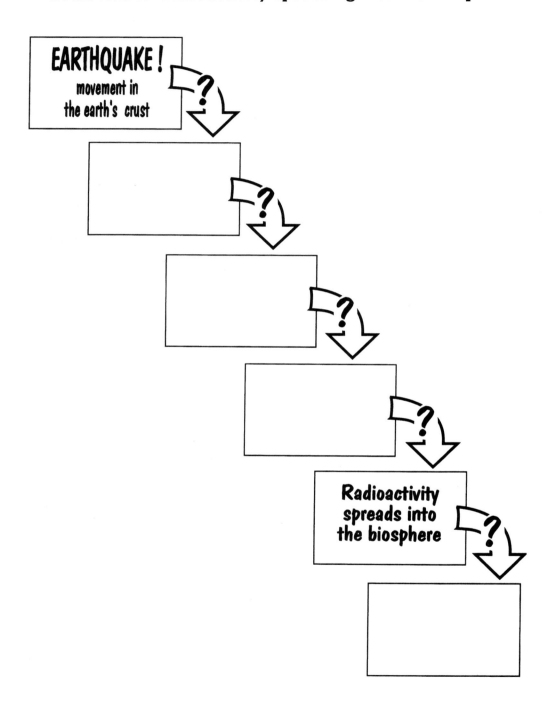

3. Do you think there is a better way for a country to dispose of its nuclear waste? Write your ideas on the lines below. Then discuss them with your classmates. Make a list of the class's solutions. Then continue reading the article.

_____

_____

_____

_____

_____

A Nuclear Graveyard *(continued)*

by Betsy Carpenter
U.S. News & World Report

Much has been made of this scary scenario by the
15   state of Nevada, which is fighting the federal
government's plan to bury all the nation's high-level
nuclear refuse inside Yucca Mountain. But in fact, the
risk to Nevadans may be overstated. Increasingly, experts view this arid, desolate ridge as a good spot for a
20   permanent nuclear graveyard. The threat to Americans
posed by the federal government's bungled attempts to
find a safe burial site for the waste looms large, however. Thousands of tons of highly radioactive spent
fuel rods rest temporarily today in pools of water—
25   some dangerously overcrowded—near nuclear power
plants around the country. At the nation's weapons
factories, corroding tanks are leaking nuclear poisons
into the ground water. This stalemate over nuclear
waste is strangling the nuclear power industry, and ex-
30   perts are increasingly troubled by the possibility that
nuclear waste could become the weapon of choice for a
new breed of terrorist.
The twin virtues of the Yucca Mountain site are its
remoteness and aridity. From the summit, the only sign
35   of civilization is the dusty trace of a dirt road cutting
across a brown, barren valley. The ridge is located on
the southwest corner of the Nevada Test Site, where the
government explodes nuclear weapons, so access is
tightly restricted. Sagebrush, creosote bushes and other
40   desert plants attest to the locale's remarkable dryness.
Indeed, only six inches of rain fall on the mountain
each year, and most of the moisture evaporates, leaving
as little as one fiftieth of an inch to soak into the ground.
The water table is unusually deep, more than one third of
45   a mile below the surface. According to the Department of
Energy, which is charged with building the repository,
nuclear waste could be buried far beneath the ground yet
still rest safely above the ground water.

50   **Geological Turmoil**
The landscape also provides stark reminders of why
critics are so concerned. To the southeast stands

Busted Butte, a peak that was sheared in half long ago
by earthquakes; to the west, four smooth-sloped volca-
55 noes rise out of a high valley. The reason for the geological turmoil is that immense forces inside the earth
are stretching the earth's crust apart here, much like a
sheet of rubber. Earthquakes relieve the strain, but they
also disrupt the water table: As the crust snaps back
60 into shape, rocks contract, and water that has seeped
deep into fractures is forced up toward the surface.

The repository site must be capable of isolating
atomic waste for 10,000 years. By all accounts, there
could be a frightful mess if the poisons escaped the
65 site. By the year 2,000, the nation will have produced
48,000 tons of high-level nuclear waste, the most con-
centrated products of the nuclear era. Every speck of
this refuse is intensely poisonous.

Water is the worst enemy of buried nuclear waste. If
70 water did find its way into the repository, it would cor-
rode the storage canisters and hasten the escape of radioactive particles through the rock. Scientists cannot
know absolutely whether ground water will well up under Yucca Mountain during the next 10,000 years. The
75 calculation simply has too many unknowns: A new ice
age, global climate change, erosion, volcanoes and
earthquakes all could affect the water table. To gauge
the probabilities, scientists reconstruct the past. If the
water table has risen in the past, scientists assume, it
80 is likely to do so again.

Jerry Szymanski, a maverick engineering geologist
with the Department of Energy (DOE), claims that he has
rock-hard evidence that ground water was once as much
as 500 meters higher than it is today. He has devoted
85 the past seven years to blowing the whistle on what he
believes to be a fatally flawed site, and his arguments
have received extensive media attention. Szymanski
bases his case largely on the presence of thick, cream-
colored veins of a crystalline deposit, known as calcite,
90 that plunge through the mottled, grey bedrock of Yucca
Mountain. In Szymanski's view, these calcite bands must
have been deposited slowly, layer by layer, as mineral-
rich ground water welled up into fractures in the rock.
"Ground water will rise again in the next 10,000 years,"
95 he says flatly. "It is as certain as death."

Other Voices

But according to an increasing number of earth scientists, it is not the site but Szymanski's conclusion that is fatally flawed. Largely as a result of Szymanski's warn-
100 ings, the National Academy of Sciences convened a panel of researchers to evaluate the risks associated with ground water. The panel has not yet released its final report, but already many members are convinced that there is no evidence for Szymanski's hypothesis—but
105 there are several good reasons to doubt it. Most believe that rainwater, not upwelling ground water, probably produced the calcite veins. One strong reason to suspect precipitation, says Bob Fournier, a geologist with the United States Geological Survey in Menlo Park, Califor-
110 nia, is that the calcite veins around Yucca Mountain do not exhibit the common structural characteristics of ancient springs. For instance, upwelling water typically leaves snowy-white mounds of calcite on the ground, deposits that are formed when the water evaporates; few
115 such signatures can be found at Yucca Mountain.

Preliminary chemical analyses also suggest that the disputed calcites were deposited by rainwater. Doug Rumble, a geochemist at the Carnegie Institution in Washington, D.C., analyzed several existing studies of the
120 chemical character of the disputed Yucca Mountain veins, the ground water underneath and ancient and modern ground water deposits; he found no evidence that the calcites at Yucca are or ever were caused by ground water.

Somewhat surprisingly, scientists are much more
125 concerned about ground water seepage than they are about more dramatic geologic events like volcanoes and earthquakes. Fresh eruptions from the small volcanoes along Yucca Mountain's western flank probably wouldn't threaten the repository because the flows would be
130 small and localized, most geologists believe. The possibility of a direct hit, a new upwelling of magma right beneath the repository, is minute, they say.

Earthquakes are not a major concern either, scientists contend. Though Yucca Mountain is ringed with
135 seismic faults, many of them known to be active, most geologists do not worry that shock waves from an earthquake could rupture the repository. Experience with tremors throughout the world has shown un-

equivocally that tunnels and mines stand up well to
140 them. For instance, a devastating earthquake killed
250,000 people in a coal-mining city in China in 1976.
Reportedly, workers in the mines below did not feel
even the slightest tremor. Closer to home, underground nuclear explosions on the nearby test site have
145 shown that tunnels can withstand forces even greater
than those produced by earthquakes.

   "From what we know now, I would feel quite comfortable with Yucca Mountain," says George Thompson,
a geologist at Stanford University and a member of the
150 National Academy of Sciences' panel. Though panel
members agree that a lot more study is needed, most
do not believe that the geological complexity disquali-
fies the site. Explains Clarence Allen, a geologist from
Caltech in Pasadena, California, "If you asked me to
155 find a site with fewer earthquakes or volcanoes, I
could. But an overall better site? I'm not so sure."

   Maintaining the pretense of an unassailable site also
has had an unfortunate impact on the design of the repository. Currently, the DOE plans to build a complex
160 that would be backfilled and sealed off after it had
been loaded to capacity. Experts like Stanford's George
Thompson assert that this approach is foolish. Instead,
the government should design the facility so that the
waste could be easily retrieved if the repository failed.

165   Congress must have had an inkling that forcing the
project on Nevada might not work out in the end. In
the same bill that designated Yucca Mountain the sole
candidate for site evaluation, Congress established the
Office of the U.S. Nuclear Waste Negotiator, which is
170 charged with finding a willing state or Indian tribe[1] to
host the repository. David Leroy, who took the job last
summer, is putting together a package of incentives
and assurances that he hopes will lure several state or
tribal leaders to the bargaining table. The assurances
175 include promises of local participation in deciding how
the facility is operated and the freedom to back out of
the evaluation process at any time. When it comes to
incentives the sky's the limit. Highways? Airports?

---

[1] In the United States, Indian (Native American) tribes own their land, called
reservations. The tribe holds decision-making power as to what takes place on
tribal land. They are not under the jurisdiction of the federal government or of
the government of the state in which the reservation is located.

180 Schools? Harbor cleanups? "You tell me what the problem is and let's see if we can address it," he says. Who knows, maybe Leroy can find a way to make even cynical Nevadans willing to host the repository.

• A. Reading Overview: Main Idea, Details, and Summary

Read the passage again. As you read, underline what you think are the most important ideas in the reading. Then, in one or two sentences, write the main idea of the reading. *Use your own words.*

Main idea:

_____

_____

_____

Details:

Use the chart below to organize the information in the article. Refer back to the information you underlined in the passage as a guide. When you have finished, write a brief summary of the reading. *Use your own words.*

A Nuclear Graveyard

The Nuclear Repository Controversy: To Use or Not to Use the Yucca Mountain Site	
Arguments Against Using This Site	Arguments in Favor of Using This Site

Summary:

_____

_____

_____

_____

_____

• B. Statement Evaluation

Read the following statements. Then scan the article again quickly to find out if each sentence is **True (T), False (F),** or an **Inference (I).**

1. _____ Experts believe that the Yucca Mountains are a good place to bury nuclear waste.

2. _____ There is a great deal of rain in the mountains every year.

3. _____ The greatest danger to nuclear waste is water.

4. _____ The presence of calcite has led to many arguments about the safety of the Yucca Mountains as a nuclear waste repository site.

5. _____ Earthquake tremors are always felt deep below the surface of the earth.

6. _____ Most members of the National Academy of Sciences' panel believe that the Yucca Mountain site may be a good place for nuclear waste disposal.

7. _____ Some Indian tribes live near the Yucca Mountains.

• C. Reading Analysis

Read each question carefully. Either circle the letter or number of the correct answer, or write your answer in the space provided.

1. In line 14, what does **this scary scenario** refer to?

   _____

   _____

2. Read lines 17–20.

   a. **"The risk to Nevadans may be overstated." To overstate** means
      1. to make something seem greater than it really is
      2. to make something seem smaller than it really is

   b. Who are **Nevadans?**

      _____

3. Read lines 33–40.

   a. **Remote** means
      1. close to people
      2. far away from people

   b. How do you know?

      _____

   c. In this paragraph, what is a synonym of **aridity?**

      _____

4. Read lines 41–48. What is a **repository?**

   a. nuclear waste
   b. a safe place for the nuclear waste
   c. the ground water above the nuclear waste

5. Read lines 62–68. What word is a synonym of **waste?**

   _____

6. Read lines 69–80.

   a. Why do scientists reconstruct the past?
      1. to try to predict what may happen in the future
      2. to help them understand the past

   b. **"It is likely to do so again"** means

      1. there may be more earthquakes
      2. the water table may rise again
      3. the climate may change again

7. Read lines 81–87. **Blowing the whistle** means

   a. making music
   b. giving false information
   c. revealing the truth

8. Read lines 105–112. What is one type of **precipitation** referred to in these lines?

   _____

9. Read lines 124–132.

   a. In this paragraph, what is another way of saying **lava flow from a volcano?**

      _____

   b. **"The possibility of a direct hit . . . is minute"** means

      1. there is a very small chance
      2. there is a very big chance

10. Read lines 133–146.

    a. **Unequivocally** means

       1. probably
       2. definitely
       3. slightly

    b. What is an example of the **unequivocal** evidence that tunnels and mines are not damaged by earthquakes?

       _____

       _____

11. Read lines 165–171.

   a. What is the job of the Office of the U.S. Nuclear Waste Negotiator?

   _____

   _____

   b. In this sentence, **charged with** means

      1. to be made to pay for something
      2. to be suspected of a crime
      3. to be given responsibility for something

12. Read lines 171–182.

   a. What are some of the **incentives** David Leroy may offer?

   _____

   b. What are some of the **assurances** David Leroy may offer?

   _____

   c. An **incentive** is a

      1. guarantee
      2. motivation
      3. freedom

   d. An **assurance** is a

      1. guarantee
      2. motivation
      3. freedom

   d. **To lure** means to

      1. attract
      2. buy
      3. discourage

   e. **The sky is the limit** means

      1. he won't agree to build airplanes
      2. he will agree to construct tall buildings
      3. anything is possible

• D. Dictionary Skills

Read the entry for each word, and consider the context of the sentence from the passage. Write the number definition that is appropriate for the context on the line next to the word. Write the entry number too when appropriate. Be prepared to explain your choice.

Part 1

1. With regard to incentives, such as highways, airports, schools, or harbor cleanups, David Leroy said, "You tell me what the problem is and let's see if we can **address** it."

   address: _____

   ad·dress \ə-'dres, a- *also* 'a-ˌdres\ *vb* [ME *adressen,* fr. MF *adresser,* fr. *a*- (fr. L *ad*-) + *dresser* to arrange — more at DRESS] *vt* (14c) **1** *archaic* **a :** DIRECT, AIM **b :** to direct to go : SEND **2 a :** to direct the efforts or attention of (oneself) ⟨will ∼ himself to the problem⟩ **b :** to deal with : TREAT ⟨intrigued by the chance to ∼ important issues —I. L. Horowitz⟩ **3** *archaic :* to make ready; *esp* : DRESS **4 a :** to communicate directly ⟨∼es his thanks to his host⟩ **b :** to speak or write directly to; *esp :* to deliver a formal speech to **5 a :** to mark directions for delivery on ⟨∼ a letter⟩ **b :** to consign to the care of another (as an agent or factor) **6 :** to greet by a prescribed form **7 :** to adjust the club preparatory to hitting (a golf ball) **8 :** to identify (as a peripheral or memory location) by an address or a name for information transfer ∼ *vi, obs :* to direct one's speech or attentions — **ad·dress·er** *n*

2. Experts view Yucca Mountain, which is an arid, **desolate** ridge, as a good spot for a permanent nuclear graveyard.

   desolate: _____

   des·o·late \'de-sə-lət, 'de-zə-\ *adj* [ME *desolat,* fr. L *desolatus,* pp. of *desolare* to abandon, fr. *de-* + *solus* alone] (14c) **1 :** devoid of inhabitants and visitors : DESERTED **2 :** joyless, disconsolate, and sorrowful through or as if through separation from a loved one **3 a** : showing the effects of abandonment and neglect : DILAPIDATED **b :** BARREN, LIFELESS ⟨a ∼ landscape⟩ **c :** devoid of warmth, comfort, or hope : GLOOMY ⟨∼ memories⟩ *syn* see ALONE — **des·o·late·ly** *adv* — **des·o·late·ness** *n*

3. The Office of the U.S. Nuclear Waste Negotiator is charged with finding a willing state or Indian tribe to be a **host** for the repository.

host: _____

¹**host** \\'hōst\\ *n* [ME, fr. OF, fr. LL *hostis,* fr. L, stranger, enemy — more at GUEST] (14c)   **1 :** ARMY   **2 :** a very large number : MULTITUDE
²**host** *vi* (15c) : to assemble in a host usu. for a hostile purpose
³**host** *n* [ME *hoste* host, guest, fr. OF, fr. L *hospit-, hospes,* prob. fr. *hostis*] (14c)   **1   a :** one that receives or entertains guests socially, commercially, or officially   **b :** one that provides facilities for an event or function ⟨our college served as ∼ for the basketball tournament⟩   **2   a :** a living animal or plant affording subsistence or lodgment to a parasite   **b :** the larger, stronger, or dominant member of a commensal or symbiotic pair   **c :** an individual into which a tissue, part, or embryo is transplanted from another   **3 :** a mineral or rock that is older than the minerals or rocks in it; *also* : a substance that contains a usu. small amount of another substance incorporated in its structure   **4 :** a radio or television emcee   **5 :** a computer that controls communications in a network that administers a database

4. Thousands of tons of highly radioactive **spent** fuel rods rest temporarily today in pools of water near nuclear power plants around the country.

spent: _____

spent \\'spent\\ *adj* [ME, fr. pp. of *spenden* to spend] (15c)   **1   a :** used up : CONSUMED   **b :** exhausted of active or required components or qualities often for a particular purpose ⟨∼ nuclear fuel⟩   **2 :** drained of energy or effectiveness : EXHAUSTED   **3 :** exhausted of spawn or sperm ⟨a ∼ salmon⟩

Pronunciation Guide

\\ə\\ **abut**   \\ˀ\\ **kitten,** F **table**   \\ər\\ **further**   \\a\\ **ash**   \\ā\\ **ace**   \\ä\\ **mop, mar**
\\au̇\\ **out**   \\ch\\ **chin**   \\e\\ **bet**   \\ē\\ **easy**   \\g\\ **go**   \\i\\ **hit**   \\ī\\ **ice**   \\j\\ **job**
\\ŋ\\ **sing**   \\ō\\ **go**   \\ȯ\\ **law**   \\ȯi\\ **boy**   \\th\\ **thin**   \\t͟h\\ **the**   \\ü\\ **loot**   \\u̇\\ **foot**
\\y\\ **yet**   \\zh\\ **vision**   \\á, k̲, ⁿ, œ, ō̵e, ue, ū̵e, ʸ\\

Part 2

Sometimes a word not only has different meanings; it also has different pronunciations depending on the meaning. For example, in this chapter, the words **minute** and **refuse** each have several meanings and two different pronunciations. Read the entries for these words carefully, and choose the most appropriate definition for the context. Check with your teacher to make sure that you pronounce the words correctly, depending on the meaning.

5. The possibility of a direct hit by an earthquake, and a new upwelling of magma right beneath the repository, is **minute**, according to scientists.

minute: _____

¹min·ute \'mi-nət\ *n* [ME, fr. MF, fr. LL *minuta,* fr. L *minutus* small, fr. pp. of *minuere* to lessen — more at MINOR] (14c) **1** : a 60th part of an hour of time or of a degree : 60 seconds **2** : the distance one can traverse in a minute **3** : a short space of time : MOMENT **4 a** : a brief note (as of summary or recommendation) **b** : MEMORANDUM, DRAFT **c** *pl* : the official record of the proceedings of a meeting
²minute *vt* min·ut·ed; min·ut·ing (ca. 1648) : to make notes or a brief summary of
³mi·nute \mī-'nüt, mə-, -'nyüt\ *adj* mi·nut·er; -est [L *minutus*] (ca. 1626) **1** : very small : INFINITESIMAL **2** : of small importance : TRIFLING **3** : marked by close attention to details *syn* see SMALL, CIRCUMSTANTIAL — **mi·nute·ness** *n*
¹re·fuse \ri-'fyüz\ *vb* re·fused; re·fus·ing [ME, fr. MF *refuser,* fr.

6. The U.S. government plans to bury the nation's high-level nuclear **refuse** inside Yucca Mountain in Nevada.
    By the year 2,000, the nation will have produced 48,000 tons of high-level nuclear waste. Every speck of this **refuse** is intensely poisonous.

refuse: _____

¹re·fuse \ri-'fyüz\ *vb* re·fused; re·fus·ing [ME, fr. MF *refuser,* fr. (assumed) VL *refusare,* perh. blend of L *refutare* to refute and *recusare* to demur — more at RECUSE] *vt* (14c) **1** : to express oneself as unwilling to accept ⟨~ a gift⟩ ⟨~ a promotion⟩ **2 a** : to show or express unwillingness to do or comply with ⟨*refused* to answer the question⟩ **b** : DENY ⟨they were *refused* admittance to the game⟩ **3** *obs* : GIVE UP, RENOUNCE **4** *of a horse* : to decline to jump or leap over ~ *vi* : to withhold acceptance, compliance, or permission *syn* see DECLINE — **re·fus·er** *n*
²ref·use \'re-ˌfyüs, -ˌfyüz\ *n* [ME, fr. MF *refus* rejection, fr. OF, fr. *refuser*] (14c) **1** : the worthless or useless part of something : LEAVINGS **2** : TRASH, GARBAGE
³ref·use \'re-ˌfyüs, -ˌfyüz\ *adj* (15c) : thrown aside or left as worthless

• E. Critical Thinking

Read each question carefully. Write your response in the space provided. Remember that there is no one correct answer. Your response depends on what **you** think.

1. Does Betsy Carpenter, the author of this article, believe that there are sufficient reasons for not using Yucca Mountain as a nuclear waste site? Explain your answer.

_____

_____

_____

2. Jerry Szymanski, who is a geologist, and "a number of earth scientists, also geologists," disagree on the interpretation of the same evidence, i.e., the calcite veins in the bedrock of Yucca Mountain. Why might Nevadans be unhappy with these conflicting interpretations of the same data?

_____

_____

_____

3. According to the article, "The repository site must be capable of isolating atomic waste for 10,000 years," the length of time the waste material remains radioactive. What implications might you draw from this concern that the site remain intact for the full 10,000 years that it remains contaminated?

_____

_____

_____

4. Does the government believe that most people would be willing to have a nuclear repository in their state? Explain your answer.

_____

_____

_____

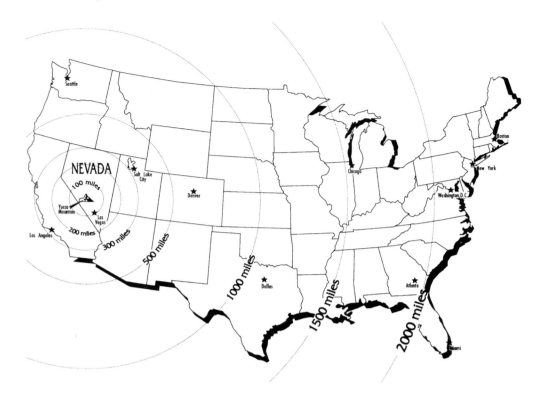

• Another Perspective

A Nuclear Graveyard (*excerpt*)

1   The biggest problem at Yucca Mountain may be local
opposition fomented in part by federal mishandling of
the site-selection process. Nine years ago, Congress
passed the Nuclear Waste Policy Act. In 1983, the DOE se-
5 lected nine sites around the country for consideration as
a possible repository. A couple of years later, the list was
narrowed down to three—Yucca Mountain, Hanford,
Washington, and Deaf Smith County, Texas. Then, in
1987, Congress ordered the DOE to focus solely on Yucca
10 Mountain, a move that Nevadans feel was made for political reasons: Nevada has one of the smallest delegations
on Capitol Hill.[1] Today, anti-dump sentiment runs deep.
Fully four out of five Nevadans oppose the project.

[1] Capitol Hill, in Washington, D.C., is the site of the Capitol building, where
Congress, consisting of the Senate and the House of Representatives, meets to
make laws. The number of representatives each state has is based on its population so that the least populated states have the fewest representatives and
consequently, less voice in the House.

Nevadans are also unnerved by the DOE's horrible
15 environmental record and long-standing culture of secrecy. Indeed, billions of gallons of radioactive and
toxic materials were dumped secretly over the past few
decades at weapons factories around the country. According to a recent report by the Congressional Office
20 of Technology Assessment, the DOE's two-year-old effort to clean up the mess left on and under DOE weapons facilities is proceeding abysmally.

Changing Benchmarks
25   In their own defense, DOE officials argue that it is
unfair to judge past practices by today's more stringent
environmental standards. Moreover, they say the Yucca
Mountain project has many layers of external oversight,
unlike the weapons facilities that were cloaked in se-
30 crecy from the start. The DOE has a point. Every aspect
of site evaluation will be scrutinized by the Nuclear
Waste Technical Review Board, a panel of experts rec-
ommended by the National Academy of Sciences and
appointed by the President. Ultimately, the facility will
35 be licensed by the U.S. Nuclear Regulatory Commission.
   But Nevadans have a case when they argue that
their state has much to lose and little to gain by host-
ing the site. With its booming economy, Las Vegas
doesn't need the 3,000 jobs the facility would provide
40 during construction. Also, a nuclear accident, even a
minor one, could harm the Silver State's gaming-based
economy by keeping tourists away.
   Many critics believe that the very notion of a site
that could be "safe" for 10,000 years is ridiculous, and
45 this has intensified local opposition. Science simply
cannot prove that a site will be safe for such a long period of time, and citizens know it and feel as if they are
being conned, says Frank Parker, chairman of the National Academy of Sciences' Board on Radioactive Waste
50 Management. Parker holds that a more honest—and in
the end more reassuring—assessment that the government could have offered Nevadans is that the likeli-
hood of a catastrophic breach is very slim and that the
DOE is prepared to act swiftly if problems occur.

• Questions for "A Nuclear Graveyard" (excerpt)

1. According to Nevadans, why was Yucca Mountain chosen as the best site for the repository? What does the author imply when she says that Nevada has one of the smallest delegations on Capitol Hill?

_____

_____

_____

2. Why do many people in Nevada oppose the dumping of nuclear waste in that state? What are their concerns?

_____

_____

_____

3. How has the DOE said it would handle the Yucca Mountain situation differently than it handled other projects (for example, weapons facilities) in the past?

_____

_____

_____

4. What business does the economy of Nevada depend on? How might this business be affected by nuclear dumping?

_____

_____

_____

• F. Follow-up Activities

1. Refer to the **Self-Evaluation of Reading Strategies** on the next page. Think about the strategies you used to help yourself understand "A Nuclear Graveyard." Check off the strategies you used. Evaluate your strategy use throughout the book. Which strategies have you begun to use consistently? Which strategies have you added to the list? Which strategies are becoming automatic? To what extent have you applied these strategies to other reading you do?

Self-Evaluation of Reading Strategies

Strategies	"Playing with Fire"	"Wilder Places for Wild Things"	"A Nuclear Graveyard"
	Readings		
I read the title and try to predict what the reading will be about.			
I use my knowledge of the world to help me understand the text.			
I read as though I *expect* the text to have meaning.			
I use illustrations to help me understand the text.			
I ask myself questions about the text.			
I use a variety of types of context clues.			
I take chances in order to identify meaning.			
I continue if I am not successful.			
I identify and underline main ideas.			
I connect details with main ideas.			
I summarize the reading in my own words.			
I skip unnecessary words.			
I look up words correctly in the dictionary.			
I connect the reading to other material I have read.			
I do not translate into my native language.			

2. Look carefully at the illustration below. Read the sentences describing how a nuclear reactor operates. Then match the sentences to the appropriate letter in the illustration.

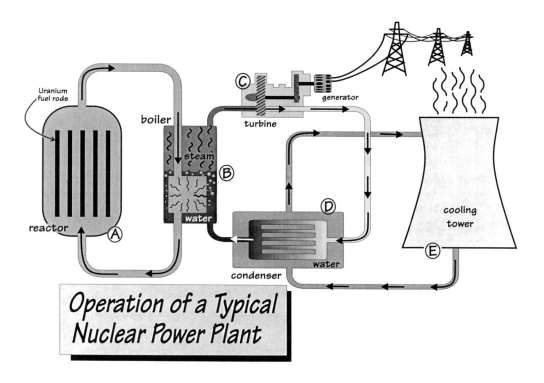

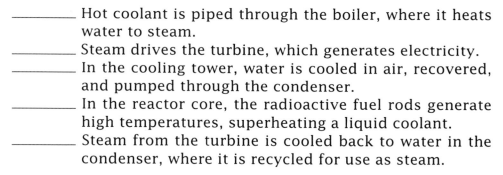

Operation of a Typical Nuclear Power Plant

_____ Hot coolant is piped through the boiler, where it heats water to steam.

_____ Steam drives the turbine, which generates electricity.

_____ In the cooling tower, water is cooled in air, recovered, and pumped through the condenser.

_____ In the reactor core, the radioactive fuel rods generate high temperatures, superheating a liquid coolant.

_____ Steam from the turbine is cooled back to water in the condenser, where it is recycled for use as steam.

3. Work in two groups. If your class is large, divide into an even number of groups. The first group will represent the Office of the U.S. Nuclear Waste Negotiator. This group will make a list of incentives and assurances to convince the other group to allow the government to build a nuclear repository in their state. The second group will represent the citizens of the state where the government wants to bury nuclear waste. This group will make a list of their concerns and demands. When the lists are completed, the students from both groups will discuss how to negotiate and compromise so that both groups are satisfied.

• G. Topics for Discussion and Writing

1. Work in pairs or small groups. Look carefully at the following chart. What observations can you make about the number and location of nuclear power plants throughout the world? Write a composition describing your conclusions.

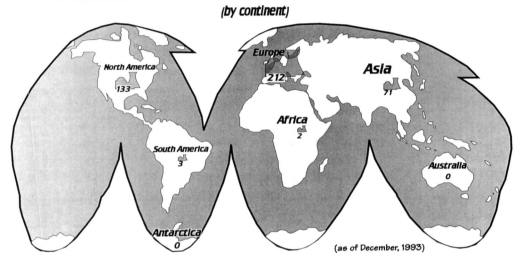

NUMBER OF COMMERCIAL NUCLEAR POWER PLANTS
(by continent)

North America
133

Europe
212

Asia
71

Africa
2

South America
3

Australia
0

Antarctica
0

(as of December, 1993)

2. If the government wanted to bury a nuclear repository in your state or province, how would you feel? Why? Write a letter to the editor of your local newspaper either in favor of or against the government's proposal.

3. In what other ways can governments dispose of nuclear waste? Discuss your ideas with your class. When you are finished, write a composition. Which ideas do you think are best? Explain your viewpoint.

4. **Write in your journal.** Do you think that the disposal of nuclear waste should be the responsibility of an individual country, or do you think this is a global issue? Explain your reasons. You may also want to discuss whether *all* environmental issues, including the destruction of rain forests, are the joint concern of all countries.

Unit IV Review

• H. Crossword Puzzle

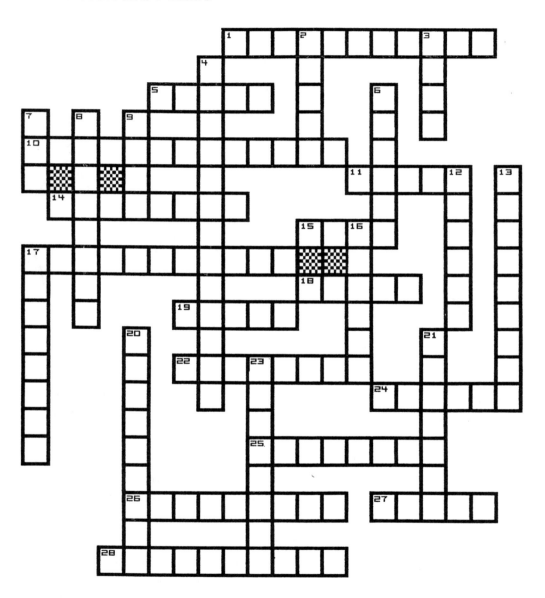

• Crossword Puzzle Clues

Across

1. increase greatly in number
5. newly arrived; just come
10. definitely
11. imitate closely
14. furthermore
15. exaggerated claims or publicity
17. not paying attention
18. search through or over
19. the careful examination of a phenomenon or development
22. an organized effort to promote or attain an end
24. far away from people; distant
25. an animal that hunts other animals for food
26. a guarantee
27. used up; consumed
28. a storage site

Down

2. flatten
3. very dry
4. the destruction of a forest
6. do something as a favor
7. a prompting as a signal to do something
8. deserted
9. attract
12. mountain lion
13. a motivation
16. provoke; cause something
17. about to happen
20. make something seem larger than it really is
21. engross; absorb
23. a pachyderm

Index of Key Words and Phrases

Answer Key

Chapter 1: Dressing for Success

A. Reading Overview: Main Idea, Details, and Summary

Main idea: The writer describes a California school district's decision to mandate a uniform dress code. The article includes arguments for and against dress codes in schools.

Details:
Arguments in favor:
President Clinton: Student uniforms promote safety and discipline in public schools.
President Clinton: Teenagers may stop killing each other over designer jackets.
A school district survey: Violence and discipline problems decrease.
Dick Van DerLaan, a school district spokesman: Parents may excuse their children from the requirement.
Ms. Moore, principal of Will Rogers Middle School: More formal clothing puts students in the right mind-set to learn.
School leaders: Uniforms make it easier to spot people who may not belong on campus.
District officials: Parents can buy uniforms at a reasonable price.
Nick Duran, an 8th-grade student and the student-body president at Rogers Middle School: People judge students on their inner characteristics rather than what they wear.
Arguments against:
Hector Gonzalez, a 7th-grade student at Rogers Middle School: Some students feel like they are in jail.
Alicia Nunez, an 8th-grade student at Franklin Middle School: Uniforms stifle students' creativity.
The American Civil Liberties Union of Southern California: Many parents cannot afford the cost of school uniforms.
Some Long Beach students: Uniforms are monotonous and dampen students' personal style.

Summary: This article describes the Long Beach school district's new policy, which requires students to dress in uniform fashion. School officials have observed a decrease in school violence as a result of the dress code. Requiring students to wear uniforms also has other benefits. However, some people have argued against this policy, for both economic and creative reasons.

B. Statement Evaluation

1. F
2. T
3. I
4. F
5. I
6. I

C. Reading Analysis

1. a. 3
   b. 2
2. b
3. a. They have the option of excusing their children from the school uniform requirement.
   b. 1
4. It is a requirement that students wear color-specific, and sometimes style-specific, clothing.
5. a
6. limits
7. b
8. a. No
   b. He feels like he's in jail.
9. Uniforms might cost more than parents can afford.

10. a. No
    b. Stepped-up parent involvement and additional conflict-resolution classes
    c. 1
    d. 3

D. Dictionary Skills

1. 5a
2. 2c(1)
3. 2a; 2a includes the idea of power; it is more specific than 1.
4. 1b; 1b includes the concept of opposition, which 1a does not.

E. Critical Thinking

Answers will vary.

Questions for "Uncool in School"

1. Answers will vary.
2. The list will vary. It might include the idea of school image. Adults such as business executives are in favor of the dress code. They seem to feel a dress code prepares students for the work world. Principals and teachers are unhappy about the dress code, in addition to the students and civil liberties lawyers mentioned in "Dressing for Success." They doubt whether the dress code is really necessary.
3. Answers will vary. The *Education Week* article includes statistics and focuses on school safety. In *The New York Times*, the article is written in a more informal style, and doesn't have such specific information.

F. Follow-up Activities

1. Responses will be individual.
2.–4. Answers will vary.

G. Topics for Discussion and Writing

Answers will vary.

Chapter 2: My Husband, the Outsider

A. Reading Overview: Main Idea, Details, and Summary

Main idea: Marian Hyun, a Korean American woman, describes her experiences with her family's reactions to her dating and marrying a non-Korean man.
Details:
Marian: Marian wanted to marry a man of her own choice. She did not want to marry a traditional Korean man.
Marian's father: Her father wanted her to marry a Korean man. He wanted her to get married when she was 24. He wanted her to have a big wedding so he could invite many friends and relatives.
Marian's mother: Her mother wanted her to marry a Korean man. She wanted to help Marian choose a husband.
Marian's aunt: Her aunt wanted her to marry a Korean man. She wanted her to get married before she became too old. She didn't acknowledge that Marian was dating a non-Korean man.
Marian's husband: Marian did not give us any information about her husband's opinion.
The Korean doctor: He seemed to feel that Marian should behave as a native-born Korean and follow Korean traditions. He probably felt that she should always agree with her husband.
Summary: The narrator, Marian Hyun, describes her experiences with her family as she dated and got married. As an American-born Korean, she had many cultural conflicts with her parents, other relatives, and the Korean men she dated. She finally married a non-Korean man and had a small wedding.

B. Statement Evaluation

1. F
2. I
3. F
4. T
5. T
6. I

C. Reading Analysis

1. b
2. b

3. the husband of a person's daughter; a person's son through marriage
4. a. 2
   b. 3
5. a. 3
   b. 2
6. a. He hounded her for 3 months.
   b. 2
7. because he hadn't realized how expensive a big wedding could be, and he changed his mind about wanting a big wedding for his second daughter

D. Dictionary Skills

1. 3b
2. 4b; it includes the concept of ideal or wish (expressed in the context).
3. 3; 1 is not appropriate because there is nothing foreign in the context.
4. 2a; it includes the concept of harmonious coexistence.

E. Critical Thinking

Answers will vary.

Questions for "Unwelcome in Chinatown"

1. She feels unwelcome in Chinatown because the waiters and salespeople treat her badly.
2. Yes, her experience as an American-born Chinese seems like a typical experience because many of her American-born Chinese friends have had the same experiences.
3. Answers will vary. Some possible responses are: (1) both Marian Hyun Amy Wu were brought up in the United States as native-born Americans; (2) they both were raised speaking English, so that neither of them is fluent in their parents' native language.
4. Answers will vary.

F. Follow-up Activities

1. Responses will be individual.
2. and 3. Answers will vary.

4. a. blacks marrying whites
   b. the percent of black marriages that involve whites
   c. Asians

G. Topics for Discussion and Writing

Answers will vary.

Chapter 3: Beyond Rivalry

A. Reading Overview: Main Idea, Details, and Summary

Main idea: Siblings are a major part of each other's lives as children, but they tend to drift apart as adults. However, as they become older, siblings often become closer again.
Details:
I. Social Connections
   A. Young Adult Siblings
      1. have careers
      2. get married
      3. have children
   B. Older Adult Siblings
      1. retire
      2. get divorced or become widowed
      3. children grow up and leave home
II. Effects of Critical Events in Siblings' Lives
   A. bring siblings closer together
   B. pull siblings further apart
III. Feelings of Aging Siblings Towards Each Other
   A. 20 percent are hostile or indifferent
   B. majority feel lingering rivalry
   C. 53 percent increased contact
      1. more free time
      2. anxiety about sibling's health
      3. fewer friends and contacts
      4. need link to the past
IV. Factors Affecting Contact with Siblings
   A. proximity
   B. having a sister
V. Factors Affecting Why Siblings Don't Ask Each Other for Help
   A. sibling is equally needy or frail
   B. sibling is a safety net
   C. latent hostility

Summary: Siblings may grow apart as adults because they become involved in their careers and get married and have children. However, as siblings become older, they retire, they may lose their spouse, and their children leave home. At this time, siblings may become closer to each other or be pulled further apart by critical events in their lives, such as the illness or loss of a parent. Even when siblings do have increased contact with each other, they tend not to ask each other for help, for several reasons.

B. Statement Evaluation

1. F
2. F
3. T
4. NM
5. T
6. NM
7. F

C. Reading Analysis

1. a. 1
   b. parental sickness; parental death
2. a. 3
   b. because the man hadn't spoken to his sister in 20 years
3. b
4. b
5. a. decline
   b. a group of people who are with you
   c. 1
6. all the way in the past to the person's childhood
7. a. 1
   b. 3
8. proximity
9. a. 2
   b. loaning money, running errands, performing favors
   c. *Such as* introduces examples.

D. Dictionary Skills

1. 4
2. 1c; it involves the idea of remembering (recollection).
3. 2a *or* 2b are appropriate; 1 is too general.
4. 2; 1a, 1b, and 1c are all either legal or formal in nature.

E. Critical Thinking

Answers will vary.

Questions for Living in a Step-Family without Getting Stepped on

1. Middle children make friends faster than anyone else in the family. They tend to leave home first, and live farther away from the family than anyone else. They like to do their own thing, make their own friends, and live their own lives. Middle children are good mediators or negotiators. They learn the art of compromise. They are often the best-adjusted adults in the family.
2. and 3. Answers will vary.

F. Follow-up Activities

1. Responses will be individual.
2. Findings will vary.

G. Topics for Discussion and Writing

Answers will vary.

H. Crossword Puzzle

Across

1. exotic
4. uphold
5. clan
9. incompatible
12. panacea
13. endorsement
14. dream
19. acknowledge
20. validate
22. bond
23. sibling
24. infer
26. case

Down

1. evoke
2. option
3. kin
6. last
7. launch
8. debate

10. estrangement
11. engagement
14. diminish
15. ABC
16. mandatory
17. wedding
18. bilingual
21. solace
25. rift

Chapter 4: Who Lives Longer?

A. Reading Overview: Main Idea, Details, and Summary

Main idea: Many factors influence how long we live. Some of these factors are unchangeable, but others, such as health and psychological factors, are changeable.
Details:
Fixed Factors: A. gender; B. race; C. heredity
Changeable Factors: Health Measures: (1) don't smoke; (2) drink moderately; (3) eat breakfast; (4) don't eat between meals; (5) maintain normal weight; (6) sleep 8 hours; (7) exercise moderately.
Psychological Factors: (1) social integration; (2) autonomy; (3) stress and job satisfaction; (4) environment; (5) socioeconomic status
What you can do: A. Institute sound health practices; B. Expand your circle of acquaintances and activities
Summary: Our longevity is affected by many factors. Some of these factors, such as gender, race, and heredity, are unchangeable. However, other factors are changeable. We can take measures to improve our health—for example, get exercise and sleep 8 hours every night. Psychological factors, such as our level of autonomy, the amount of stress in our lives, and the number of friends we have, also affect our longevity, and we can change these, too.

B. Statement Evaluation

1. F
2. NM
3. T
4. T
5. NM
6. F
7. T

C. Reading Analysis

1. a. fallacies
   b. because scientists are separating two opposite ideas; the opposite of a fact is something that is not true, i.e., false—a fallacy
2. c
3. b
4. a
5. cigarette smoking, drinking, and reckless driving
6. c
7. social integration, autonomy, stress and job satisfaction, environment, socioeconomic status
8. b
9. stress and job satisfaction
10. c
11. a

D. Dictionary Skills

1. 3; 1, 2a, 2b, and 4 all refer to physical structures.
2. 3a, because it refers to intensity of quality.
3. 3, because it includes the concept of influencing an action or decision; 2 refers only to an opinion.
4. 3b is the most appropriate, given the context; 5 is also appropriate.

E. Critical Thinking

Answers will vary.

Questions for "More Senior Citizens, Fewer Kids"
1. The article discusses the declining birth rate and the increasing life expectancy in Taiwan.
2. In Taiwan, the proportion of elderly people to young people will increase steadily.
3. There will be a new set of social welfare needs such as nursing homes and day care programs for the elderly. There may not be enough young people to support older people. Because of the declining birth rate, there will be a dwindling population of working-age adults, which will slow economic growth.

4. The government had family planning campaigns. People are marrying later (at an older age), and some young people are opting to stay single.

F. Follow-up Activities

1. Responses will be individual.
2. a. This chart shows life expectancy for males and females born in the U.S. in the decades 1940–1990 and in 1993.
   b. (1) about 75 years
      (2) about 67 years
   c. (1) 1940 to 1950; males gained almost 5 years
      (2) 1940 to 1950; females gained almost 6 years
      (3) Answers will vary. Explanations in general include medical advances, *especially* the introduction of antibiotics, specifically penicillin. The polio vaccine was also developed about this time.
   d. (1) Males gained about 11 years.
      (2) Females gained about 13 years.
3. a. This chart shows life expectancy highs, lows, and averages by continent for people born in 1994.
   b. Answers will vary. Clearly, race alone does not provide an answer, since Afghanistan and Sweden have a predominantly white population, yet they represent countries with both very low and very high life expectancies. Explanations might include widespread endemic diseases, general sanitation, water quality—factors that affect entire populations.
4. and 5. Answers will vary.

G. Topics for Discussion and Writing

Answers will vary.

Chapter 5: The Mindset of Health

A. Reading Overview: Main Idea, Details, and Summary

Main idea: Our state of mind can positively or negatively affect how we respond to health issues. A mindful approach to illness can positively influence our health.

Details:

The Significance of Mindless Attitudes:
Context: We accept preconceived notions of the context of a particular situation.
State of Mind: We jeopardize our body's ability to handle a situation.
The Significance of Mindful Attitudes:
Context: We place our perception intentionally in a different context.
State of Mind: Our state of mind positively influences our state of body. For example, people who fasted for personal reasons were less hungry than people who fasted for external reasons only, such as money.
The importance of context and mindfulness in handling illness:

1. Our interpretation of the events around us could be the first link in a chain leading to serious illness.
2. There are some diseases that were thought to be physiological and incurable. They may be more under our personal control than we believe.
3. Mindful or mindless reactions to disease (such as cancer) can influence its effects.
   a. There are probably people with undiagnosed cancer who feel healthy and may remain healthy.
   b. There are people with diagnosed cancer who go into a decline that is not directly related to the disease.

Research supporting the effects of mindfulness:

1. Patients have been successfully taught to tolerate pain by seeing how pain varies depending on context. The patients needed fewer pain relievers and left the hospital earlier than a comparison group of patients.
2. People in a nonsmoking context

didn't suffer withdrawal symptoms, but they did experience craving again when they returned to a context where smoking was allowed.

How to take a more mindful approach to illness:

1. Try to heal ourselves and not depend completely on doctors.
2. Get new information from our bodies and from books.
3. Work on changing contexts, both physical environment and emotional outlook.
4. Try to stay healthy rather than be made well.

How to positively influence our health:

1. Exchange unhealthy mindsets for healthy ones.
2. Increase a generally mindful state.

Summary: We may have mindful or mindless attitudes toward illness. If we have a mindless attitude towards an illness, we tend to be accepting, and we jeopardize our body's ability to handle the situation. If we have a mindful attitude towards an illness, we can positively affect our body's ability to get well. There are several ways in which we can take a more mindful approach toward illness and positively influence our health.

B. Statement Evaluation

1. T
2. F
3. T
4. F
5. I
6. T
7. I

C. Reading Analysis

1. a. mindlessly
   b. 3
2. a. mindfully
   b. 2
   c. 1
3. a. 1
   b. an external reason
   c. The subjects who were less hungry showed a smaller increase in free fatty acid levels.
4. b
5. a. the source of pain

b. The term is defined after the dash.

6. a
7. a. the health risks, the bad smell, the cost, others' reactions to smoking
   b. the relaxation, the concentration, the taste, the sociable quality
   c. 3
8. b

D. Dictionary Skills

1. 4b; all of 1, 2, 3, and 6, as well as 4a and 4c, refer to physical objects; 5a and 5b refer to groups of people.
2. 2b; 2a is too specific; 2c implies an obligation to another; all of 1 refers to legal or formal matters.
3. 3c(1) is the most specific to the context.
4. 1a(1)

E. Critical Thinking

Answers will vary.

Questions for "How to Behave in a Hospital"

1. She suggests that we act submissive, humble, grateful, and undemanding. In other words, she suggests that we be passive.
2. We should act as if it may be our fault, but never that it might be the fault of anyone working in the hospital.
3. Gloria Emerson suggests that we take no active role in our treatment and that we do not ask questions when we don't understand. In contrast, Ellen Langer says that we should be active and ask questions to understand our medication and treatment.

F. Follow-up Activities

1. Responses will be individual.
2. to 4. Answers will vary.

G. Topics for Discussion and Writing

Answers will vary.

Chapter 6: My Genes Made Me Do It

A. Reading Overview: Main Idea, Details, and Summary

Main idea: This article describes the controversy regarding the causes of human behavior—that is, whether our personality and behavior traits may be attributed to heredity or to environment.

Details:
1. the gene for breast cancer; it is a scientifically valid discovery, but it has fallen short of initial claims
2. addiction, shyness, and even political views and divorce; these emotional disorders and behaviors are linked to claims based on statistics, not on scientific evidence
3. correlations in traits between identical and fraternal twins were examined; research showed that identical twins are treated more alike than are fraternal twins. This finding indicates that environment (nurture) is a more likely explanation for these twins' similar traits.
4. schizophrenia and manic-depression; these disorders were identified by geneticists in the late 1980s. Their findings were later disproved. In fact, it appears that these and other major mental illnesses may be due to social (i.e., environmental) factors.
5. alcoholism, anorexia, and overeating; the discovery of an "alcoholism gene" was announced in 1990. However, in 1993, Dr. Gelernter demonstrated that there was no link between this gene and alcoholism.

Summary: The issue regarding whether human personality and behavior traits may be attributed to heredity or to environment has been the subject of ongoing controversy. Claims that genetic factors have been discovered for such traits as mental illness, alcoholism, and even overeating have been disproved or severely criticized. Strong evidence exists to show that these and other traits are actually the result of social factors. In fact, it may not be possible to separate out genetics and environment (i.e., nature and nurture); further research is needed.

B. Statement Evaluation

1. F
2. T
3. T
4. NM
5. F
6. NM

C. Reading Analysis

1. a. 2
   b. being able to reverse and eliminate mental illness and to identify the causes of criminality, personality, and other basic human foibles and traits
   c. 2
   d. 1
2. a
3. a. mental illnesses like schizophrenia and depression, social problems like criminality, and personal maladies like obesity and bulimia
   b. 2
   c. 2
4. a
5. b
6. b
7. c
8. genetic, environmental

D. Dictionary Skills

1. The second full entry (the verb form): 2
2. 3c(2); 1 and 2 refer to money; the other entries are not relevant to the context.
3. The first full entry: 2, because it involves a number
4. 3b is the closest in meaning, given the context, because it refers to a change in emphasis (that is, the incidence of).

E. Critical Thinking

Answers will vary.

Questions for "Of (Fat) Mice and Men"

1. Dr. Friedman announced that he had identified a genetic mutation in obese mice, as well as a nearly identical gene in humans.
2. The mice do not sense when they have eaten enough, so they continue eating.
3. Behavioral geneticists agree only in part with these findings. They believe that less than half of total weight variation is programmed in the genes.
4. Other factors that might account for obesity in humans are the abundance of rich foods, that many Americans overeat, and that teenagers (teens) are much less physically active than they were even ten years ago.
5. Accepting that weight is predetermined might be a drawback to people because they would simply accept becoming obese. They would feel they could not control their weight.

F. Follow-up Activities

1. Responses will be individual.
2. (a) This graph illustrates the percent of overweight adults between the age of 20 and 34 in the United States, by gender.
   (b) It shows that, for the periods indicated, the percent of overweight 20–34-year-old females has steadily increased.
   (c) It shows that, for the periods indicated, except for 1976 through 1980, the percent of overweight 20–34-year-old males has steadily increased.
   (d) Answers will vary. One trend is that 20-34-year-old males are increasingly likely to be as overweight as 20-34-year-old females. Another trend is that this age group, as a whole, is increasingly likely to become more overweight in the future.

3. Answers will vary.

G. Topics for Discussion and Writing

Answers will vary.

H. Crossword Puzzle

Across
2. sound
6. versus
8. link
11. intentionally
13. commitment
14. nature
15. combat
17. landmark
21. fast
22. drawback
23. unabated
24. say
25. coronary

Down
1. course
3. notion
4. hypothesis
5. trait
7. shift
9. key
10. profound
12. automatically
16. assumption
18. discount
19. fixed
20. nurture

Chapter 7: Assisted Suicide

A. Reading Overview: Main Idea, Details and Summary

Main idea: Dr. Moore, who has been practicing medicine all his life, describes two very ill patients he treated differently. He concludes that the decision to help end a patient's life requires strong judgment and long experience.

Details:

The Dilemma: For doctors with terminally ill patients, the dilemma is whether to actively help these patients die.

Case #1: A former nurse who had sustained a fractured pelvis. Her condition was serious: her lungs filled up; her urine stopped, her heart developed dangerous rhythm disturbances. She was on life support equipment. Her family requested that the doctor take her off the machines.

Dr. Moore's decision: not to take her off the machines.

The patient's outcome: she became well.

Case #2: An 85-year-old woman whose hair caught fire. Her condition: she had a deep burn; her condition was probably fatal.

Dr. Moore's and the nurses' decision: they backed off treatment; they gave her plenty of morphine.

The patient's outcome: she died.

The lesson of Dr. Moore's experiences: As a reasonable physician, you had better do what you would want done for you. Assisting people to die requires strong judgment and long experience to avoid its misuse.

Summary: Dr. Moore, 81, has practiced medicine all his life. He describes two very ill patients he once treated differently. One he refused to let die; the other he did help die. He brought up the second patient's case at an ethics seminar where the participants were surprised that he discussed a real case. In both cases, he feels he made the right decision. He believes that the decision to help end a patient's life requires strong judgment and long experience.

B. Statement Evaluation

1. F
2. I
3. T
4. I
5. I

C. Reading Analysis

1. a. 2
   b. 3
   c. when to help a patient die
   d. 3
2. a. giving patients heavy medication so that they die
   b. 1
   c. 2
3. b
4. b
5. a. It means that patients who are in very bad condition can suddenly get better.

b. an electrical device that maintains a person's heartbeat
   c. It is described in lines 16–19.
6. the former nurse (the men's wife and mother)
7. c
8. a. 3
   b. 1
9. c

D. Dictionary Skills

1. 2c, because it refers specifically to the principles governing a profession.
2. The second full entry: 1a; the past participle of *fracture* used as an adjective to describe something broken.
3. 1 **or** 4b are appropriate, given the context.
4. 6b

E. Critical Thinking

Answers will vary.

Questions for "Should Doctors Be Allowed to Help Terminally Ill Patients Commit Suicide?"

1. a. Humphry believes that death is part of medicine and that doctors should be able to help terminally ill people die if their suffering becomes unbearable.
   b. Depressed people should be counseled and helped to live.
2. Answers will vary. Humphry's wife might have asked her doctor to help her end her life, and he might have done so, because Humphry stated that there was nothing *else* they could do.
3. Callahan believes that doctors should never help terminally ill people die. If they want to die, they can commit suicide without a doctor's assistance.
4. He worries that people will be pushed to suicide by a doctor's suggestion. He also worries that people will be pushed by their families because of the medical expenses and the burden to their families.

F. Follow-up Activities

1. Responses will be individual.
2. and 3. Answers will vary.

G. Topics for Discussion and Writing

Answers will vary.

Chapter 8: Sales of Kidneys Prompt New Laws and Debate

A. Reading Overview: Main Idea, Details, and Summary

Main idea: In an effort to control the sale of organs for transplant, Britain and other countries have passed laws prohibiting the sale of organs. Some people fear that these laws may lead to fewer available organs for transplant.
Details:
Laws about organ donation:
Britain: It is a criminal offense to sell or buy organs
World Health Organization: Does not make laws governing the sale of organs.
U.S.: The sale of human organs is unlawful.
Belgium: According to law, organ donation is automatic upon death, unless specifically requested otherwise.
Opinions about sales of organs:
Britain: It is a controversial issue in Britain.
World Health Organization: It condemns the practice and has asked member nations to take appropriate measures, including legislation, to prohibit trafficking in human organs.
U.S.: Ethicists and policy analysts have suggested that paying donors or their estates may be an effective way to increase the supply of available organs.
Belgium: We have no information about Belgian opinions.
Arguments in favor of a law prohibiting the sale of organs:
1. Instead, legislation should include making organ donation automatic upon death (in order to increase organ availability).
2. People in desperate circumstances have, and would, sell their organs, even martyr themselves, in order to save their families.
3. Some people would sell an organ for frivolous reasons.
4. The law could scare off donors (who might see any kind of donation as improper).
Arguments against a law prohibiting the sale of organs:
1. People should be able to do whatever they wish with their bodies, if it's of their own free will.
2. A monetary thank-you could stimulate increases in organs and tissue available for transplantation and research.
Summary: Because many people, especially poor people, have been selling their organs for transplants, Britain, the United States, and other countries have passed laws prohibiting the sale of organs. However, some people fear that such laws may lead to the decrease of available organs for transplant. In addition, other people do not object to the sale of organs.

B. Statement Evaluation

1. F
2. F
3. T
4. T
5. NM
6. F
7. NM
8. T

C. Reading Analysis

1. a. 2
   b. 1
2. a. selling human organs for transplant
   b. 2
3. c
4. a. Britain's National Health Service
   b. 1
5. a. 1
   b. 3
6. a
7. c
8. a. 1
   b. to buy Porsches (i.e., cars) or take a girlfriend on a holiday
   c. 2

D. Dictionary Skills

1. 2b; 2a is also appropriate
2. 2c
3. a. 1c
   b. 3a
4. The second full entry: 2

E. Critical Thinking

Answers will vary.

F. Follow-up Activities

1. Responses will be individual.
2. a. This graph compares the number of heart, lung, kidney, liver, and pancreas transplants in the United States for the years 1982 and 1995.
   b. (1) kidney
      (2) kidney
      (3) Kidney transplants are the most frequent because people have two kidneys. Two kidneys are available from a cadaver. In addition, kidneys are more available from living donors as well as from cadavers because people can live with one kidney.
   c. (1) kidney
      (2) liver
3. Answers will vary.

G. Topics for Discussion and Writing

Answers will vary.

Chapter 9: The Gift of Life: When One Body Can Save Another

A. Reading Overview: Main Idea, Details, and Summary

Main Idea: Faced with the terminal illness of their daughter, the Ayala family decided to have another child in order to provide a compatible donor. The Ayalas' decision generated considerable controversy regarding the ethical and moral issues involved in their case and similar ones.

Details:
The Ayalas' Dilemma: their daughter Anissa was terminally ill; her only brother's marrow was incompatible with hers.
The Ayalas' Decision: to reverse Abe Ayala's vasectomy and to have another child to serve as donor for Anissa.
Arguments Supporting the Ayalas:
(1) They would be able to save their daughter's life. (2) It makes just as much sense to have a child to save another as it does to have a child for any other reason. (3) They will love the second daughter, and would not have aborted her even if she had not been a suitable donor.
Arguments Opposing the Ayalas:
(1) It is not ethical to bring a baby into the world to serve as a biological resupply vehicle. (2) The baby did not consent to be used as a donor. (3) The parents created a new life and used it for their own purposes.
The Larger Dilemmas:
(1) Today, life is being tapped to save life. (2) What is the morality involved if a couple conceives a baby for such a purpose and the fetus's tissue is incompatible? Do they abort the fetus and try again?
(3) Is the risk for living donors worth the chance of saving another's life?
(4) Could the body be turned into a commodity if compensation is offered for organs?
Summary: The Ayalas' decision to conceive a child as a donor for their daughter has caused concern and controversy. Ethical concerns include the morality of giving life to a child who will serve as a donor without giving its consent, the issue of abortion if the fetus proves to be an incompatible donor, the issue of living donation and the risks to the donor, and the debate over compensation for organ donation.

B. Statement Evaluation

1. F
2. T
3. F
4. I
5. I
6. T
7. F

C. Reading Analysis

1. b
2. a
3. a. 2
   b. in cases of leukemia
4. a. 2
   b. 2
   c. 1
5. a. when the baby was old enough and strong enough to donate safely
   b. 1
6. agree
7. a
8. b
9. a. driving safety laws
   b. because fewer people die in driving accidents, so there are fewer cadaver organs available
10. a. 3
    b. 1
11. a

D. Dictionary Skills

1. 1b
2. *vt*, 1
3. The second full entry: *vt*: 2
4. 3a, because it refers to intensity of feeling

E. Critical Thinking

Answers will vary.

Questions for "Two Parents Offer Their Daughter the Breath of Life—To No Avail"

1. a. two
   b. Yes. The two lung transplants were successful. However, Alyssa died of heart failure.
2. Because either or both of his parents risked dying from their partial lung transplants.
3. a. Cindy still experiences pain. Roger suffers from muscle weakness.
   b. No, they don't.

F. Follow-up Activities

1. Responses will be individual.
2. Answers will vary.

G. Topics for Discussion and Writing

Answers will vary.

H. Crossword Puzzle

Across

2. pacemaker
4. catheter
7. organs
12. address
13. impoverished
14. automatic
19. martyr
20. practice
21. optimum
23. controversial
24. retrospect
25. case

Down

1. fatal
3. essential
5. ethics
6. donor
8. cadaver
9. deem
10. disclose
11. kin
15. maintain
16. denouement
17. frivolous
18. excerpt
22. marrow

Chapter 10: Playing with Fire

A. Reading Overview: Main Idea, Details, and Summary

Main idea: The Amazon rain forests in Brazil are being destroyed at an alarming rate. This destruction is negatively affecting the environment, and may reach a point where deforestation cannot be reversed.

Details:

I. The Destruction of the Amazon Rain Forests
   A. by loggers who cut down trees
   B. by builders of dams, which flood the land
   C. by gold miners, who poison rivers with mercury
   D. by farmers, who burn sections of the forest for farming

E. by the government, which is clearing land for highways
II. Effects of the Disappearance of the Rain Forests
   A. Over one million species of animals and plants will vanish.
   B. It may change global weather patterns.
   C. Burning the forest sends huge amounts of CO_2 into the atmosphere.
III. Overview of How Brazilian Rain Forests Became Endangered
   A. Brazil built the Trans-Amazon Highway to help settle the country's interior.
   B. Settlers cleared the land and planted crops.
   C. The poor soil failed in a few years.
IV. Advantages of Maintaining the Rain Forests
   A. The market value of jungle produce will yield more income than cattle ranching or lumbering.
   B. Rain forests are a potential food source.
   C. Rain forests are a source of alternative, natural pesticides.
   D. Many jungle chemicals may be effective drugs in treating diseases such as cancer.

Summary: In an effort to settle its vast interior, the Brazilian government built a highway to encourage people to move to and farm vast areas. However, the farmers and ranchers engaged in a process involving burning the rain forest to clear land. The poor soil eventually failed, and people have continued to clear land and destroy the rain forest. Environmentalists are concerned that the deforestation is creating serious environmental problems, and may lead to the permanent, irreversible destruction of the Amazon rain forest.

B. Statement Evaluation

1. T
2. T
3. I
4. F
5. I
6. T
7. I

C. Reading Analysis

1. a. 2
   b. because of the thousands of fires in the rain forests
2. b
3. a
4. a. 2
   b. 2
   c. because of loggers, dams, mercury pollution, and cocaine farming
5. c
6. a
7. a. the trapping of heat by atmospheric CO_2
   b. carbon dioxide
8. b
9. c
10. a
11. a British journal

D. Dictionary Skills

1. 3d
2. *vt:* 4a
3. The first full entry: 3. In the first full entry, 1 is also appropriate, given the context
4. 1d(1) because it describes the three-year analysis; 1d(2) more appropriately describes what Charles Peters actually published

E. Critical Thinking

Answers will vary.

Questions for "Taking Two Steps Back"

1. (1) Smoke blocked out the sky for hundreds of miles; (2) many people developed bronchial problems and had to be hospitalized; (3) the smoke blinded motorists and caused highway accidents.
2. Mendes was a union leader and environmentalist who protested against land-clearing ranchers. He was probably murdered to stop the protests and to frighten other people who were concerned about the environment.
3. a. As a result of the Earth Summit in 1992, Brazil backed (supported) treaties designed to protect the environment. In addition, because

of a weaker (souring) economy, ranchers did not have the money to expand.

   b. Because Brazil's economy has become much stronger (has rebounded) recently, farmers are beginning to expand again. Another reason is that a drought has made it easier to set fires and keep them going.

4. a. The government claims that the newspapers have exaggerated the extent of the fires. (The headlines are way out of proportion.)

   b. The author disagrees with the Brazilian government's explanation, because he says that "Only now has Brasilia come up with $2.4 million for a detailed survey of the last three years' damage." He implies that the government wasn't interested before.

F. Follow-up Activities

1. Responses will be individual.
2. a. This chart illustrates the destruction of the world's rain forests from 1700 through 2100.

   b. There were 1,200 million hectares.

   c. None

   d. (1) It means the rate of destruction that will probably occur in the future.

      (2) It is based on the actual rate of destruction since 1950.

      (3) We can change this rate by limiting further destruction of the world's rain forests.

3. and 4. Answers will vary.

G. for Discussion and Writing

Answers will vary.

Chapter 11: Wilder Places for Wild Things

A. Reading Overview: Main Idea Details, and Summary

Main Idea: As many species of animals are being threatened with extinction, the role of zoos has become more important. This role includes preserving endangered animals and providing naturalistic settings to encourage the animals to reproduce.

Details:

  I. Examples of Animal Behavior in Naturalistic Settings

    A. Beavers cut down trees for their winter food supply.

    B. Chimpanzees work for food by manipulating tools.

    C. Gorillas mate and form families.

  II. Zoos Re-create Animals' Natural Environment

    What zoos do: reproduce sights, sounds, feel, and smell of the wild. Examples: rainstorms; cliffs; trees, plants, jungle vines; waterfalls, natural food; artificial day and night Results: Animals mate, raise young, and develop survival skills.

  III. Species-Survival Programs (SSPs)

    A. Purpose of the SSPs

      1. To pair up males and females from different zoos.

      2. To breed endangered species.

      3. To inform and excite the public about zoos and animals.

    B. Examples of Successful Animal Releases into the Wild

      1. The return of condors to the Andes

      2. The release of golden lion tamarins into a reserve in Brazil.

      3. The return of oryxes to Oman, Jordan, and Israel

Summary: The role of zoos has become increasingly important as more animals are threatened with extinction. Zoos have begun providing more naturalistic settings, which encourage animals to reproduce, and exchanging animals for breeding purposes. Zoos preserve endangered animals and sometimes even return them to their natural environments.

B. Statement Evaluation

1. F
2. T
3. O
4. F
5. T
6. T
7. O

C. Reading Analysis

1. a. their food
   b. 1
2. mating and forming a family
3. b
4. c
5. a. because the animals' environment is not really natural
   b. 1
   c. lion-tailed macaques
6. a. elephants
   b. 2
7. species-survival program
8. a
9. c
10. a. 1
    b. 2

D. Dictionary Skills

1. The second full entry: 1b (the context does not call for a verbal signal).
2. 2
3. The third full entry: 3; 1 and 2 refer to physical actions.
4. 2b, in a more general sense, since the action is not in fact a favor.

E. Critical Thinking

Answers will vary.

Questions for "Predators on the Prowl"

1. Iris Kenna was killed by a mountain lion.
2. a. Californians must decide on a law to permit mountain-lion hunting.
   b. The purpose of the law is to control the mountain-lion population, which in California is now 6,000 animals.
   c. Some people are against the proposed law because they favor the animals; they think the animals should be protected.
3. The mountain-lion problem has increased because hunting of mountain lions has been banned since 1972. In addition, the human population has increased greatly, and people have taken over mountain-lion territory.
4. Most people in Colorado believe that development in mountain-lion territory should be restricted.
5. Answers will vary. They are probably in favor of restrictions on land development. They state that people "usurped" (a negative term) wild animal territory, and that cougars are "majestic" (a positive term).

F. Follow-up Activities

1. Responses will be individual.
2. and 3. Answers will vary.

G. Topics for Discussion and Writing

Answers will vary.

Chapter 12: A Nuclear Graveyard

Prereading Preparation

1. a
2. (1) Earthquake! movement in the earth's crust. (2) Ground water wells up suddenly, flooding the repository. (3) Nuclear poisons seep into underground water that flows to Death Valley. (4) Insects, birds and animals drink at the valley's contaminated springs. (5) Radioactivity spreads into the biosphere. (6) Disaster!
3. Answers will vary.

A. Reading Overview: Main Idea, Details, and Summary

Main idea: The U.S. government has selected Yucca Mountain in Nevada as a possible site for a nuclear waste depository. This choice has created considerable controversy.
Details:
Arguments against using the Yucca Mountain site: (1) The landscape shows evidence of earthquakes and volcanoes. (2) Earthquakes disrupt the water table. (3) Water corrodes storage canisters and hastens the escape of radioactive particles through the rock. (4) Scientists cannot know absolutely whether ground water will well up under Yucca Mountain during the next 10,000 years. (5) If poi-

sons escaped from the site, there could be a major disaster (a frightful mess). (6) If the water table has risen in the past, it is likely to do so again, especially over 10,000 years. Szymanski pointed out geological evidence to support this theory. (7) The federal government has made mistakes in the past with regard to storing nuclear waste.

Arguments in favor of using the Yucca Mountain site: (1) Geologists believe that shock waves from an earthquake could not rupture the repository. They also believe that eruptions from small volcanoes probably wouldn't threaten the repository because the flows would be small and localized. (2) Underground nuclear explosions at the nearby test site have shown that tunnels can withstand forces even greater than those produced by earthquakes. (3) The site is very remote. It is very far from civilization. (4) The water table is unusually deep. Nuclear waste could be buried far beneath the ground yet still rest safely above the ground water. (5) A panel of researchers, convened by the National Academy of Sciences to evaluate the risks associated with ground water, disagree with Szymanski's findings.

Summary: The U.S. government's possible plan to build a nuclear waste repository in the Yucca Mountains in Nevada has created considerable controversy among Nevadans (who don't want the site in their state), the Department of Energy, and the National Academy of Sciences' panel of researchers, geochemists, and geologists. These people have debated the available geological evidence, and so far no one has agreed to host the site.

B. Statement Evaluation

1. T
2. F
3. T
4. I
5. F
6. I
7. I

C. Reading Analysis

1. an earthquake causing water contamination that will poison life
2. a. 1

b. people who live in the state of Nevada; residents of Nevada
3. a. 2
   b. There is only a trace of a dirt road; obviously, almost no one lives in that area.
   c. dryness
4. b
5. refuse
6. a. 1
   b. 2
7. c
8. rain (rainwater)
9. a. upwelling of magma
   b. 1
10. a. 2
    b. Workers in a mine in a Chinese city did not feel any tremors when a devastating earthquake hit the city.
11. a. to find a state or an Indian tribe willing to host the nuclear waste depository
    b. 3
12. a. Incentives include offers to build highways, airports, or schools and to pay for harbor cleanups.
    b. The assurances include promises of local participation in deciding how the facility is operated and the freedom to back out of the evaluation process at any time.
    c. 2
    d. 1
    e. 1

D. Dictionary Skills

Part 1
1. 2b; 2a might also be appropriate.
2. 1 *or* 3b are appropriate to the context.
3. The third full entry: 1b, in the sense of providing a facility, but not for an event or a function.
4. 1b

Part 2
5. the third full entry: 1
6. the second full entry: 1

E. Critical Thinking

1. Answers will vary. However, she probably doesn't think it's a poor location because in the first

sentence of the continued article, she describes the potential disaster as a "scary scenario," which implies exaggeration. She also says, "In fact, the risk to Nevadans may be overstated." The overall tone of the article seems biased in favor of the site.

2.–4.Answers will vary. For #3, possible responses might include that the people designing the repository, as well as the U.S. government, have a sense of responsibility for people who will live in the near and distant future. The government might be concerned about legal consequences if the site contaminated the water in the foreseeable future, for instance, the next 100 or even 200 years.

Questions for "A Nuclear Graveyard"

1. The site was chosen for political reasons. The author means that Nevada, because it has a small population and, consequently, few delegates in Congress, did not have the political power to influence the decision to locate the repository in Nevada.

2. Nevadans are concerned about the DOE's horrible environmental record and long-standing culture of secrecy. Furthermore, the DOE's efforts to clean up secret dumps have failed abysmally. Nevadans are worried that the same thing might happen to them.

3. The Yucca Mountain project will have many layers of exernal oversight, and will not be kept secret.

4. Nevada's economy depends on gaming (gambling, as in Las Vegas) and tourism. The nuclear repository might keep tourists away from Nevada.

F. Follow-up Activities

1. Responses will be individual.
2. B, C, E, A, D
3. Answers will vary.

G. Topics for Discussion and Writing

Answers will vary.

H. Crossword Puzzle

Across
1. proliferate
5. fresh
10. unequivocally
11. mimic
14. moreover
15. hype
17. inattention
18. scour
19. study
22. movement
24. remote
25. predator
26. assurance
27. spent
28. repository

Down
2. level
3. arid
4. deforestation
6. oblige
7. cue
8. desolate
9. lure
12. cougar
13. incentive
16. prompt
17. imminent
20. overstate
21. immerse
23. elephant